BUYING A PROPERTY IN FRANCE

The Daily Telegraph

BUYING A PROPERTY IN FRANCE

Edited by
Philip Jones

KOGAN PAGE

The rules and regulations governing property purchase in France and other associated topics covered in this book, including national and international legislation, are constantly being reviewed and changed. Kogan Page Limited, *The Daily Telegraph* and the authors cannot assume legal responsibility for the accuracy of any particular statement in this work. No responsibility for loss or damage occasioned to any person acting or refraining from action as a result of the material in this publication can be accepted by the authors or publishers.

First published in Great Britain in 1990 by
Kogan Page Limited, 120 Pentonville Road,
London N1 9JN.

British Library Cataloguing in Publication Data
A CIP record for this book is available
from the British Library.

ISBN 0-7494-0317-9
ISBN 0-7494-0192-3 Pbk

Typeset by DP Photosetting, Aylesbury, Bucks
Printed and bound in Great Britain by
Richard Clay, The Chaucer Press, Bungay

Contents

Foreword

The formula of this book was developed during *The Daily Telegraph*'s inaugural French Property Event at Olympia in London in March 1990.

One of the features of this highly successful event was a programme of seminars offering professional advice from some of the leading authorities - in both Britain and France - on the various aspects of buying property across the Channel. This unprecedented assembly of specialist talents offered an ideal opportunity to produce a book, under the auspices of *The Daily Telegraph*, covering the full range of subjects on which these experts are so eminently qualified to comment.

The challenge was accepted with wholehearted enthusiasm, and the following pages are a reflection not only of this spirit of co-operation, but also of the willingness of the contributors to share the benefit of their experience and expertise.

The editor would like to acknowledge this *esprit de corps* and is confident that the resulting work will assist the many thousands of people who will be buying a home of their own in France.

Chapter 1
'That Sweet Enemy'

PHILIP JONES

'Having this day, my horse, my hand, my lance
Guided so well; that I obtained the prize;
Both by the judgment of the English eyes;
And of some scent by that sweet enemy, France!'
'Astrophel and Stella'

We could hardly have a better phrase to sum up our ambivalent feelings towards the French. It was over four hundred years ago that Sir Philip Sidney, Elizabethan courtier, traveller and poet, wrote these lines, but he has given us the perfect description of the inconsistent, bitter-sweet relationship that has always existed between Britain and her nearest continental neighbour.

We are fascinated by each other. We are infuriated one moment, infatuated the next. We are a constant source of mutual amusement, annoyance . . . and affection.

With increasing ease, the British and French are resolving innate differences in character and temperament to create lasting friendships and respect. 'Make friends with a French person, and you will have a friend for life.' The observation was made by a French colleague, but the compliment to her compatriots was qualified. 'The French are sometimes difficult to become friendly with at first,' she said. 'But once you have been accepted, you can return to a village twenty years later and they will still be happy to welcome you.'

It is a minor miracle in itself, of course, that in twenty years' time, our French acquaintances will still be resident in the same village. The British attitude to property makes this kind of endurance and stability somewhat difficult to comprehend. We are considerably more nomadic and regard the selling and buying of houses every few years as perfectly normal practice. Indeed, when favourable economic conditions prevail, we view it as a source of action to be highly recommended. Despite the downturn which hit the British property market in the late 1980s, home ownership remains something of a national obsession for us. The French simply do not share our passion for house-hunting, conveyancing and furniture removals.

This is but one aspect of French social life that is so different from the

British. As two advanced, sophisticated European nations, we do have much in common; but there is even more in our identities that is peculiarly our own. We may be divided by just a few miles of sea, but in many ways we are oceans apart – in our culture and customs, our attitudes and appearance, our lifestyles and language.

That is the paradox of our relationship. We are within easy reach of each other, and yet remote. At times, perhaps, we come too close for comfort. We rub shoulders so often that, on occasions, we inevitably find each other a little too abrasive.

Today's *entente cordiale* may be turbulent from time to time, but it survives. To do so, it must defy the arguments of history, as well as geography. For centuries, associations between Britain and France have been a confusion of alliance and conflict, harmony and dissension, partnership and competition.

History would hardly regard us as traditional allies. After all, we spent centuries at war with each other. Yet, those same medieval hostilities did much to awaken a national spirit in France at a time when the country was torn by internal differences and disputes.

Some would say our distinctive characteristics are the very thing which, eventually, makes the British and French compatible. Perhaps those few miles of sea are not, after all, a hindrance, but a positive encouragement to Franco-British concord. We are opposite poles attracted, irresistible rivals, for ever curious about the other. The trend may be towards a 'single' Europe, political, economic, cultural; physical barriers may be falling; but France will always be 'foreign', always a little exotic. Long be it so, for that is the precise appeal. *Vive la différence!*

Anyone who even contemplates the purchase of a home abroad must relish the prospect of adventure, of discovering something new, exciting and different. Now, the army of home-buyers heading for France is attempting what a succession of English monarchs failed to achieve: to hold on to the corner of France that they have acquired. This is not a military expedition, however, but a friendly invasion, prompted by respect for, and sympathy with, the French way of life. Despite pockets of resentment across the Channel (in some cases for perfectly understandable reasons), the indications are that it will succeed and, indeed, be well received.

Ultimately, the shape and character of the new Europe will be determined by popular trends and emerging compatibility such as this, whatever the politicians, economists and industrialists might decide for us.

It is human nature, more than any other single factor, which is responsible for our latent *camaraderie*. The history books may not exactly

From La Manche to La Riviera, from Les Alpes to L'Atlantique, Pelège Loisir have a home for you.

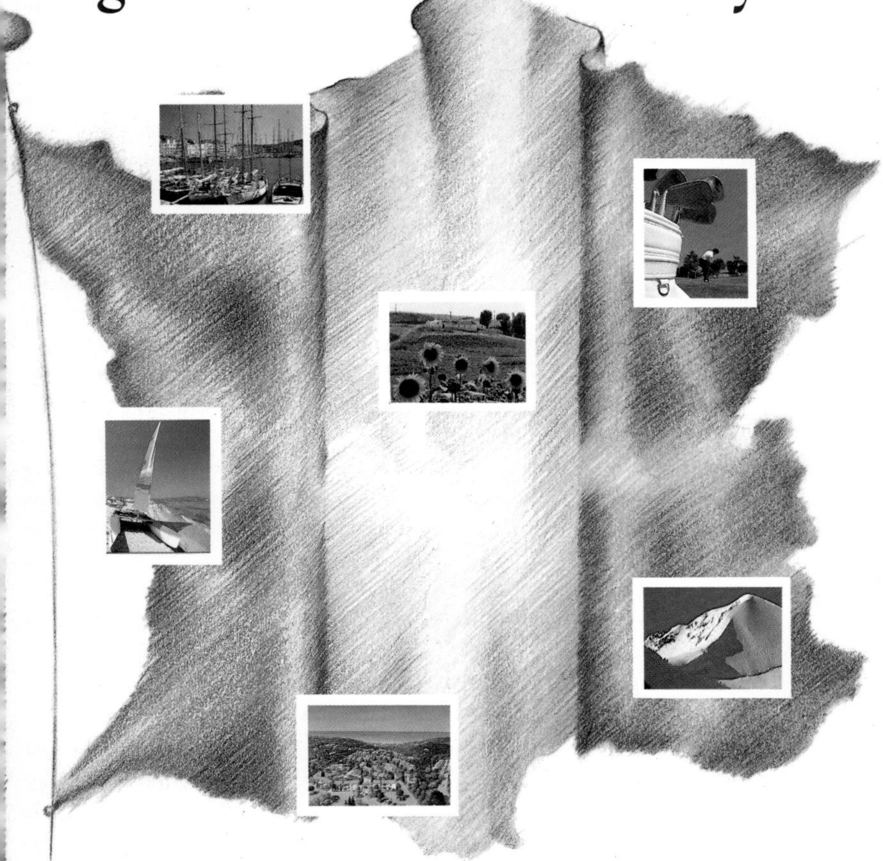

Cap Hernès, part of the Port Fréjus marina development on the French Riviera, is typical of the superb locations that Pelège Loisir have chosen for their developments. Apartments enjoy delightful views of either the sea or the marina and all are a short step from the golden sandy beach.

PELEGE LOISIR

Pelège Loisir are one of the finest construction companies in France. Their exciting new developments cover the length and breadth of the country offering quality homes for all tastes and budgets.

Crown Relocation International, the exclusive UK representatives for Pelège Loisir, skillfully match property to people. Their unrivalled service includes legal and financial advice and a thorough knowledge of the French property market.

Whatever your requirements, Pelège Loisir have a new home in France for you. Telephone or write for further information to Crown Relocation International, (Dept LRA90), 24 Market Square, Princes Risborough, Bucks HP17 0AN. Tel: (0844) 274274 Fax: (08444) 7958.

CROWN RELOCATION INTERNATIONAL

tell tales of unmitigated mutual admiration between the British and the French, but the vocabulary we use today is hardly the language of confrontation. Indeed, we do not simply 'like' France; we 'adore' it. The landscape, the villages, the cafés and restaurants are 'divine'. The food and wines are 'irresistible'. We 'love' the lifestyle.

We British, quizzically regarded by our continental neighbours as the epitome of *sang-froid*, suffer an uncommon rush of blood when we even think of France. Once there, and we are captivated by the *ambiance*; we are smitten by the sheer romance of the place. No sooner are we on the other side of the Channel than our attitudes change and we lose some of our most deeply rooted national characteristics and instincts.

For almost a decade, we British have been obsessed with the notion that we are what we eat. The result of this intensive programme of dietary re-education is evident at breakfast tables around the country. For many of us, white bread is most definitely out of favour. Once we set foot in France, however, we can hardly wait to dive into the nearest *boulangerie* to acquire a whole metre of the stuff! What a difference a ferry makes. All of a sudden, the *baguette* is the best thing since sliced bread.

Similarly, many of our French visitors, hardly the most fervent champions of British culinary skills, cannot resist the temptations of the traditional Great British fry-up the moment they arrive on our side of the Channel!

The truth, perhaps, is that both nations are more flexible and keen to adjust than we give ourselves credit for.

Whatever the reasons, the fact is that more and more Britons are discovering the pleasures of France every year, and we are not alone. The appeal of the French way of life and the many and varied attractions of coast, countryside and capital are drawing visitors from all over the globe. The French government puts the total number at 40 million a year, with almost nine million of these coming from Britain.

France has long been a popular holiday choice, of course, but improved communications have made her more widely accessible. Nowadays, our destination is not simply Paris or one of the fashionable resorts. Indeed, many visitors deliberately choose to avoid them, heading off the beaten track to discover fresh delights around the remote corners of the country.

There is something for everyone. France still reflects the diversity of her past. There may be a strong national identity today, but local character also plays an important part in everyday life alongside those qualities that are essentially French. After all, France is the largest country in western Europe, so there is ample room to accommodate regional tastes and variations.

These are rich and plentiful – not just in the people and their culture, but also in the scenery and climate, flora and fauna, food and drink and architectural style. The variety is inexhaustible: glorious sandy beaches and sparkling seas, rocky headlands and imposing cliffs, lush pastures and enchanting river valleys, awesome alpine peaks and dramatic gorges, orchards and vineyards bursting with fruit, bustling towns and quiet rural retreats, beautiful half-timbered houses, fabulous *châteaux*, functional resort apartments and dilapidated farm buildings.

A wet, windy winter's day in the north of France is likely to be just as disagreeable as it would be in England. However, we do not have to travel too far south before we can start to enjoy a milder, gentler climate, leading to long, warm spring and summer days.

The pleasures of France assault our senses the moment we arrive – the taste of the coffee and croissant in the boulevard café, the sights and sounds of the market-place, where the stalls are brimming with vegetables and cheeses, the sumptuous offerings of the restaurants, not forgetting, of course, the aroma of freshly baked bread in the *boulangerie*!

Is there any wonder then, that so many francophiles are no longer content with just an annual fleeting visit to sample all this? Is it not perfectly understandable that an increasing number should want a place in France that they can call their own?

A home in France

The overseas home owner is by no means a novelty in France. At the beginning of 1990, it was estimated that more than 120,000 British people already owned a property there, with a further 100,000 expected to join them within three years. In the past, foreign buyers traditionally tended to head south, seeking the sun in Provence, the Riviera or Dordogne. For those who preferred a shorter journey, Deauville and Le Touquet in the north were often popular choices. Since 1988, a growing number of people have become aware of the attractions and value of French property, regarding a purchase not just as a desirable course of action, but also as one which is well within their capabilities. As a result, there has been a boom in sales, with today's generation of buyers keen to explore every nook and cranny of France to find the house of their dreams, and local agents having to adapt to serve this new market and its particular demands.

These developments have helped to create a whole new business and professional structure on both sides of the Channel. More and more legal practices throughout Britain are being consulted for advice on property transactions in France. Solicitors have been diving for the covers – and the contents – of *Lefèvre*'s highly respected tome to brief themselves on the detailed texts of the French Civil Code. There has been a substantial growth in the number of organisations offering French property for sale and information on how to finance and complete a purchase. France was once the province of a handful of specialist agents, serving comparatively few clients who were interested in selected parts of the country. Now, there are hundreds of agents selling houses all over France to a vast clientèle. They vary from those who have chosen to concentrate on a particular region, to those who combine their French service with their normal operations in the British property market.

Accountants and consultants are being called on more frequently to advise on the financial and fiscal considerations of owning a property or running a business in France. Some of these professionals have decided to move to France themselves to serve this growing demand. There has been an increase in the number of organisations offering translation services and language courses. There are even companies specialising in 'house-sitting', who will look after your property for you, tending the garden, supervising renovation or conversion projects, managing holiday letting arrangements on your behalf, maintaining the building and generally keeping an eye on the place while you are away.

Other business people and professionals whose activities are directly related to housing and land have been setting up in France as well. Surveyors, architects, builders, roofing contractors and interior designers are among those who have established a base in France to be near British home buyers requiring their services. This development could not have been more opportune. It has offered many people the chance to consolidate and even expand their operations, just when the property recession in Britain was becoming an increasingly serious threat to the well-being of their businesses.

The love affair with French real estate is by no means a purely British phenomenon, however. France is internationally attractive. French estate agents report a growing interest not only from people in other European countries such as Holland, West Germany and Scandinavia, but also much further afield. As well as developing links with their British counterparts, many of these agents have been establishing contacts in the United States, Japan and Hong Kong.

The tax implications of buying a property in France are dealt with elsewhere in this book. Suffice it to say at this point that many countries, including Britain, benefit from a double tax treaty with France. Residents of countries which have this arrangement are eligible for certain fiscal agreements and protection in relation to their property in France. Special care must be taken by the residents of those countries which do not have such a treaty – and these include the Channel Islands. These advantages will not be available to them.

There are many reasons for the widespread interest in property in France, apart from the sheer joy of sharing in the French way of life. For many people, the size of the country is a great attraction. France is twice as large as Britain with roughly the same population. There are wide expanses of open countryside, offering breathing space and the chance to get away from it all and find peace and quiet.

This tranquillity may be an increasingly elusive luxury in many parts of Britain, but it is still temptingly close. France is accessible; and that, too, is an important consideration. The Channel Tunnel will bring the north of the country within even easier reach, particularly of people who live in south-east England. In response to this new challenge, ferry operators and airlines are improving their services to continental destinations and introducing special facilities for customers who own a property across the Channel.

Once you are in France, transport is excellent, with high speed train services and a rapidly developing network of motorways and other roads enabling you to travel quickly and efficiently from one part of the country to another.

Financial considerations

French property has become more accessible from the financial point of view as well. Despite the slump in the UK market, triggered by escalating interest rates, the 1980s witnessed a sharp overall rise in house values in most parts of Britain. For this reason, prices in France compare extremely favourably. You can still find property for £10,000, or even less, if you are prepared to carry out major renovations. At the other end of the scale, there are extensive estates, country houses of great architectural value and character, restored manor houses or splendid, spacious *châteaux*, often costing no more than a suburban three- or four-bedroom house in many parts of Britain. For buyers who are interested in a particular type of holiday, or who are concerned about the problems of long-distance maintenance and security, there is an ever-increasing number of purpose-built developments to choose from along the extensive coastline of France or in the mountains.

If you need to borrow in order to buy your house in France, various options are available. Lending institutions in several countries have reacted to the explosion of interest in French property, and offer a range of loans in francs, sterling or other currencies. These are constantly beind modified and updated, and serve, once again, to bring the home in France within wider reach.

The French banks are only too willing to open accounts for overseas buyers, and provide various facilities, including direct debit and standing order arrangements. The relaxation of exchange controls between Britain and France in 1990 has made the transfer of funds between the two countries a relatively simple operation. However, you may still prefer to do this through the formal banking system, should you ever need to prove exactly how much money you took into France and for what purpose.

For most people the house in France will continue to be a holiday home or regular weekend retreat, but for others it will represent a complete change of lifestyle, a new start in a new country. Age is immaterial. Many regard France as the ideal place in which to retire. First-time buyers, too, who perhaps cannot afford to acquire a home of their own in Britain, are taking advantage of the lower property prices to step on the housing ladder for the first time.

There are those, who, in accordance with the new spirit of enterprise in Europe, are benefiting from the relaxation in trade and industrial restrictions to find employment or start a business of their own in France. For some purchasers, French property is intended purely and simply as an investment - commercial as well as personal. Many British builders have been seizing the opportunity to buy land for development or old and derelict buildings for renovation.

No one, though, should regard investment in French property as the way to make a fast fortune. Prices are generally too stable for that. Before you even start to show a profit, any increase in value will first have to cover the additional costs of purchase (significantly higher in France than in Britain) as well as any expenses incurred in restoring or modernising the property.

Supply and demand

Prices have been going up, it is true, prompted in parts of the country by foreign demand. However, it will take far greater overseas involvement in the French real estate market than even the current phenomenon is providing if the overall trend is to change dramatically. External influences have to be particularly strong if they are to have a marked effect on domestic conditions. If there is not a vigorous local demand, foreign activity alone can hardly be expected to cause a steep increase in prices.

The French market is not subject to the volatile swings that are so characteristic of the British property scene. In Paris, other large cities and the fashionable resorts, notably on the Côte d'Azur, prices do rise quite sharply. This, however, is more the result of constant French demand, rather than massive foreign interest. Parts of the north, where British buyers have been most active in the last few years, have also seen above average increases. In general, however, house prices in France rise slowly and steadily.

In most rural areas, supply outstrips demand. French farming tradition has created an apparently inexhaustible crop of attractively priced properties to tempt the overseas buyer: beautiful country houses, cosy cottages, ruined farm buildings.

For centuries, France has been a predominantly agricultural country, but the contribution of agriculture to the national economy is diminishing, and mechanisation has had a significant effect on the labour requirement. The inevitable result has been a migration to the towns and suburbs, and the abandonment of many, now redundant buildings – houses, as well as barns. Traditionally, the French prefer to live near their work. While Britons yearn for a place in the country, commuting is an aspect of modern life which the French tend to shun. So, if their employment is now in a town, they will also choose to live there.

Thousands of country properties require complete restoration. Many of those on the market have been unoccupied for several years. Some are ruins with little or no sanitation. Generally speaking, these are of no great interest to the local population, although they are often precisely what the British buyer is looking for.

As we have already seen, our French counterparts do not move house as frequently as we do and, when the children marry, they often choose to build a new house on the family land. In this way, the demand for existing properties on the market is less intense than in the United Kingdom.

The complexity of French inheritance laws has also contributed to the supply of available property. Estates are often passed down to a large number of beneficiaries, with the result that many properties are then divided up and sold. This was precisely one of the aims of the French Revolution and the intention of the architects of the *Code Civil*: to break up the large estates of the aristocracy. As in so many other areas of French life, the effects of those Revolutionary measures are still being felt today.

Social integration

You are unlikely to make a quick profit through your home in France. Buying into the lifestyle should be the real investment. That lifestyle should become your own, too, at least when you are in France. You will derive the maximum pleasure and enjoyment from your property only if you are prepared to become a part of the community in which you have chosen to live - permanently or temporarily. If you respect and sympathise with the wishes of the local residents, you will be accepted quickly. Show some tangible evidence of your willingness to integrate. Make your own contribution to the economy of the town or village by using the local shops, market, garage and restaurants. After all, if you are spending time in France, amid such wonderful gastronomic delights, what is the point of loading the boot of the car with the food you are used to at home?

Be friendly. Adapt. Remember, life will not be exactly the same as it is in Britain. Do not expect British attitudes - social, cultural, economic or legal - to apply. They will not.

In some instances, there might be resentment if demand for secondary homes pushes up prices to the point where local people can no longer afford to buy a house themselves. However, this is not a common situation, certainly at present. Not only is property readily available in many areas, but also the houses that British buyers in particular are seeking are often the very ones that the French do not want for themselves. Indeed, many French people are only too pleased to see houses that have been empty for several years lived in and looked after once again.

There is little point in creating British cliques in France, when France, presumably, was the original attraction. Make the effort to speak French. It will be appreciated. Attempt to chat to your neighbours in their own language. After all, you have chosen to stay in their country. Ask them for advice and recommendations, should you need a plumber or an electrician. Again, there is perhaps someone in the village who will be only too pleased to look after your home in your absence.

Remember, too, that with 40 million foreigners setting foot in France each year, the French people are accustomed to receiving visitors. They are also great conversationalists, so make the first move. You are very likely to meet that friend for life!

Chapter 2
Home Truths and Homework

PHILIP JONES

Philip Jones is a BBC Television producer, who has made documentaries highlighting the growing interest of British people in France, French property and the French way of life.

Buying a new home, wherever it is, can be both an exciting and a daunting prospect. For most of us, it is an enormous investment. There are complex issues to be considered, even when the purchase is in our native country, let alone in one where the legal, financial and fiscal systems, the language and the social customs and attitudes are all different from our own.

During the time you spend house-hunting in France and the three or four months it might then take to complete, you will find yourself asking scores of questions on a whole range of topics. You may turn to a number of people for help and advice on the transaction itself and your subsequent ownership of the property. These sources of information will include not only the professionals who are involved in the selection, financial and conveyancing procedures, but also the 'everyday' experts - individuals, like yourself, who have already bought a home in France and who may be only too willing to share their personal experiences with you.

The most important questions, however, are those which you ought to be asking yourself from the outset. This critical self-appraisal should identify your motives for buying in France, what you hope and aim to do with the property and whether you will make full use of it. By the time you actually start to look for a house, you should have thought about and solved certain problems, such as:

Why do we want to buy a house in France?
Where, exactly, do we want to be?
What type of property do we want?
Realistically, is it right for us?
Can we afford it?
Do we need a mortgage?

If so, should we borrow in French francs, sterling or another currency?
Can we afford to keep up the repayments?
Can we afford to restore it?
Can we afford the regular upkeep?
Who will look after it while we are away?
Will it be secure in our absence?
Will we make regular use of it?
Is it too far away?
Can we afford to go over to France regularly?
Have we the time to go to France regularly?

When you have satisfied yourself that you wish to proceed, there is still much you can do before you even set foot in France on your first house-hunting visit.

Homework

In many respects, buying a house in France is less complicated and less stressful than it is in most parts of Britain. To begin with, there is less chance of being gazumped!

The Civil Code

Conveyancing in France is strictly governed by law, with considerable provision for consumer protection. It is a written law. The French love paperwork, and that can be an enormous benefit and comfort to the overseas buyer. Most of the paperwork will be handled by the *notaire*, who must supervise and authenticate all property transactions if they are to be legal and valid. The terms of the Civil Code, handed down from Napoleonic times, are there for everyone to see and refer to. Of course, there are exceptional cases but generally, the procedure is well controlled, efficiently practised and not something to be intimidated by. There are certain similarities in the French and British conveyancing procedures but, as we shall shortly discover, there are also important differences in this, as in so many other aspects of our everyday lives. There are areas of difficulty and potential pitfalls to trap the unwary and the unaware.

For that reason, you should spend time at home familiarising yourself with the French system, with the terms that will be used and with the professionals you will meet during the course of the transaction. Learn as much as possible about all of this before you arrive in France. Prepare in good time. The more you can do as early as possible, the better your chance of a smooth, worry-free transaction.

Personal documents

Look out not only your passports, but also your birth certificates and marriage certificate. The *notaire* will want to see these documents and possibly divorce papers too, if applicable, before you can complete. This is not simply a means of verifying your identity and status, but is also related to the intricacies of French inheritance law. You should draw up a will, if you have not yet done so. The reasons are explained in Chapter 7 where the whole question of inheritance in France is discussed at length.

Loans

If you will require a loan, contact your bank or building society as soon as possible. You will have to decide in which currency to borrow. If you choose a French lender, that same consumer protection legislation means you will not be able to accept the loan offer within ten days of receiving it. This compulsory 'cooling-off' period is for your benefit, but it does mean that the process will be held up. In all, you should allow at least ten weeks for your money to come through.

In processing your loan application, the lender will want details of your income and existing financial commitments. Have the information ready in good time. Try to find out before you go to France how much you might be allowed to borrow, and how much it will cost you each month to repay your loan.

When you are deciding how much you want to pay for a property, bear in mind that the French banks will lend you a proportion (normally up to 80 per cent) of the basic purchase price only. This means you will have to finance the fees, taxes and other costs incurred in the transaction out of your own resources, and it could come to as much as a further 20 per cent.

If you decide to borrow in French francs, you are likely to be offered a fixed rate of interest for the duration of the loan – normally no more than twenty years – although there are also schemes which offer variable interest rates. When deciding between a francs or sterling loan, you will have to weigh the exchange rate risk of borrowing in one currency, when your income is in another, against the uncertainty of volatile interest rates which are a feature of the sterling mortgage.

Bank account

It is advisable to open a French bank account as soon as you decide to buy. You can do this in Britain or France. It is a straightforward procedure, and will simplify enormously the payment of electricity, water, gas and local tax bills, as well as your mortgage commitments.

When you come to transfer funds into your French bank account, again allow plenty of time. It could take longer than you expect for the money to reach your account and to be cleared, and if you go overdrawn without prior arrangement you could find yourself forbidden to operate a bank account in France for a year!

Estate agents

Contact several British estate agents who deal with property in France. Choose agents who have strong French connections. Study the details of a variety of properties so that you can gain some appreciation of what is available at what price. Examine the whole range of houses in and around your price bracket - their type, quality, condition and exact location. When consulting a British agent, check the commission arrangements. Most will share the fee with their French colleagues and you ought not to be asked to pay commission twice.

Most British agents will organise your visits to France for you, putting you in contact with their associates across the Channel and arranging appointments for you to view the houses that are of interest. Apart from offering you advice on the selection of your property, the agent should also monitor your eventual transaction, helping to smooth its progress and avoid delays.

Periodical publications

National newspapers are another source of valuable information. Several carry regular features on buying a home overseas, along with advertisements for property in France - and, indeed, elsewhere. The new wave of interest in French housing has prompted the launch of various magazines dedicated to the subject. These are produced in English by publishers on both sides of the Channel, and also contain advertisements of properties throughout France.

Location

Before you start to view properties, try to define, as closely as possible, what you are looking for, where, and how much you are prepared to pay. As we have seen, the selection of houses available in France is so enormous that if you are to give yourself a fair chance when it comes to the viewing stage, you should already have identified certain basic criteria and priorities. Unless you have narrowed the field in advance, you simply may not be able to cope with the number of houses to be viewed.

In deciding where to buy, you will most likely draw on your personal experiences from previous visits to France. Unless you have a particular area definitely in mind, consider all the options. Since the fees, taxes and additional costs of purchase are considerably higher in France than in Britain, a mistake at this stage will not only be regrettable, but expensive, too. Study the maps; read up about the regions which interest you; discuss and think carefully about the various possibilities . . . then go over and have a good look around.

On the spot

It is worth recognising, from the start, that you are likely to need more than one visit in order to find and select the property that is right for you. When planning your visits, ensure that you allow yourself sufficient time in France. Consider making a preliminary trip simply to familiarise yourself with the locality. Ideally, you should see the area you have chosen at various times of the year – certainly during the winter. Time your house-hunting carefully. Holiday periods may suit your diary, but they are also the time when the offices of many French agents and *notaires* are closed.

For the same reason, unless you have made definite appointments before you set off, you could find that a weekend is equally unsuitable. The chances are that it will not be long enough. Again, when you are in France visit several agents. The number of houses you arrange to view may depend on your energy and the amount of time at your disposal. On the one hand, too many properties might blur into one confusing image by the end of your stay. On the other, unless you happen to be lucky early on, you will need to see enough properties to be able to build up an accurate picture of what is good value and what is not.

Be realistic about what you can achieve each day. In planning your itinerary, do not underestimate how long it will take to travel from one house to another, particularly if you are driving around the countryside. Allow enough time, too, at each location, so that you can inspect the property thoroughly.

Professional status of *notaires* and agents

In France, you could find your house not only through an estate agent, but also through the *notaire*, who, in addition to his legal responsibilities, is also permitted to offer properties for sale. This is another legacy of French farming and countryside tradition. It dates back to the time when, in isolated rural areas, farmers wishing to sell real estate would ask the *notaire* to find a buyer for them and handle the transaction from start to finish.

The professions of *notaire* and estate agent are strictly regulated in France. As well as being an independent professional, the *notaire* is a public officer responsible to and controlled by the Ministry of Justice. He must follow a code of conduct and sign a personal insurance covering his professional responsibility.

Agents must have a professional qualification and also a financial guarantee enabling them to receive the deposit you pay when you sign the initial contract. They must display in their offices the number of their professional charter, which has to be renewed annually, and the sum of their financial guarantee with details of the organisation which covers it. If the sum of the guarantee is less than FF500,000, the agent is not entitled to receive your deposit. Instead, it should be paid to a *notaire* or other lawyer. Many agents belong to a professional association, such as FNAIM (*Fédération Nationale des Agents Immobiliers et Mandataires*) or SNPI (*Syndicat National des Professionnels Immobiliers*).

In addition, French agents must receive a mandate from the vendor, authorising them to offer the property for sale on his or her behalf. This authorisation should also state the agent's commission and who is responsible for paying it. In some parts of France it is the vendor who pays; in others, the purchaser; in some areas the cost is shared. It is always advisable to check. Unlike the *notaire*'s commission, which is called the negotiation fee, that of the estate agent is not fixed by law. It tends to be higher than the *notaire*'s, and is generally between 4 and 8 per cent, although in some cases it could be as high as 10. So shop around. If there is a difference in the asking price of the same house offered by two or more estate agents, ask why.

In France the agent, as well as the 'consumer', is protected in law. Once you have been offered a property by the agent you cannot then attempt to cut him out of the proceedings by dealing directly with the vendor. The agent would be protected by a penal clause, making you liable to pay him not only the commission, but also an additional sum to the same value.

What the price includes

When you are house-hunting in France, you may find that the same property is being offered at an apparently lower price by the *notaire* than by the agent. This is because the agent normally includes his commission in the price he quotes, whereas the *notaire* does not. Again, do check; and if you negotiate a lower purchase price, be clear that the new, revised figure is still inclusive. So establish the price of the property, the cost of any fixtures and fittings and additional land that may be included, the commission (and who is to pay it), the legal fees and taxes that are due and the mortgage costs - the monthly payments and any arrangement fee.

Property details

Many French agents do not display the houses on their books as prominently as their British counterparts. Often there is no photograph and the description of the property contains few details. Marketing techniques are beginning to change, however, particularly among those who are working closely with agents in Britain.

If it will help you to recall particular details of a property or to distinguish between all the various houses you might view during the course of your visit, take along a notebook and camera. If you have not been able to reach a decision while you are in France, and you return home to think things over, you may well find a photographic and written record of your visit extremely useful.

The French agent will take you round the houses you choose to view, and you may wish to supplement the record you keep of your visit by marking a map with the precise location of each property. The *Institut Géographique National* produces an excellent range of highly detailed maps showing the locality of many buildings.

The *notaire*'s role

Whatever route you take to find and select your property, whether it is through a *notaire*, an agent or even from the vendor, it is the *notaire* who will eventually supervise the completion of the transaction. It is important, therefore, to appreciate what his responsibilities are.

The *notaire*, who is referred to as *Maître*, and whose office is known as an *étude*, is authorised by the State to ensure that the law of France is applied - by and to everyone concerned. He must also see that all taxes due to the State on completion of the deal are paid. It is often erroneously believed that the *notaire* legally represents both the vendor and the purchaser. He does not. He represents neither. He works on behalf of the government of France.

The *notaire*, therefore, does not defend your particular interests. In Britain, we are used to having our own legal representative during the process of conveyancing. This is not an automatic feature of the French system. The *notaire* will make the necessary enquiries and searches on the property with the local authority and the Land Charges Registry. He will verify that the property is the vendor's to sell and that there is no outstanding loan against it of a greater value than the current purchase price. He will also check any pre-emption rights, entitling official authorities and organisations representing the farming industry (such as

SAFER, *la Société d'Aménagement Foncier et d'Etablissement Rural*) to step in and buy the land or building instead of you.

In many straightforward cases, the system may well take care of itself and you too, as long as the rules are followed. However, if you feel you have particular circumstances which warrant attention or, indeed, if you are in doubt about anything to do with the transaction, seek professional advice sooner rather than later.

The *notaire*, for example, will not make the kind of extensive local searches specifically on your behalf that your solicitor in Britain would do. Without carrying out your own, independent enquiries, therefore, you might not know until after you have bought your property that a new road is to be built nearby. It is certainly worthwhile visiting the *cadastre*, the local survey office, where plans showing the current lie of the land are held for public inspection. For future developments, go to the *Département de l'Urbanisme* in the *mairie*, or town hall. This is the equivalent of the local council planning office in Britain. In any case, you should consider going along to introduce yourself to the mayor. His powers are far more wide-reaching than those of his British counterpart. He is a vital source of local information and the person who has the authority and responsibility to make many decisions which might affect your property.

Talk to other residents in the neighbourhood; go to the local café and chat with the customers and the proprietor. They will all have intimate knowledge of the area and may well be aware of any developments being planned in the locality.

Equally, although he is not your formal legal representative, ask the *notaire* if you are unsure of anything. If the mayor is the person with the detailed local information, the *notaire* is the one who has the legal expertise.

You are perfectly within your rights to appoint a second *notaire* to supervise the completion. In these circumstances, you will not pay the *notaire*'s legal fee twice. Both officials will share the one fee. However, if you instruct your own *notaire* to carry out specific enquiries and other duties on your behalf, you may well have to pay him for this, as you would any other independent legal representative.

Professional advice

In selecting your property, you may feel that you also need the professional help of a surveyor. The structural survey is, perhaps, a peculiarly British practice. We certainly feel more comfortable about buying an older property if an inspection has been carried out. The French, however, do not appear to share our concerns. In France, there is no direct equivalent of the British chartered surveyor. The French banks do not even insist on a valuation of the property when they consider your application for a loan. Instead, they are more interested in your ability to keep up the repayments.

However, there are various French professionals who will inspect your property for you. You could consult an *architecte*, a building contractor, an *expert géomètre* or an *expert immobilier*; the *expert géomètre* is the person to call in to deal with matters relating to the land, perhaps to define the boundaries of your property. It is quite common in France to be able to negotiate the amount of land to be included in the transaction.

More British chartered surveyors are now practising in France, too. They need to have professional indemnity insurance, which should be extended to cover their work across the Channel.

The decision whether to instruct a British surveyor or a French professional must eventually be your own, of course. Some people prefer to have technical documents, such as a structural report, written in their own language. Others consider the detailed local knowledge of the French expert, accumulated over a number of years, to be an overriding advantage.

If you are buying a country property in an isolated area, you can always install new plumbing and drainage. What you must check, however, is that there is an existing supply of water.

If the house needs renovating, you can apply for a second loan to help to cover the cost of this. You will need quotations to submit with your application. Your agent, surveyor, French building professional or 'house-minding' organisation can offer local advice and assistance, and if you are unable to spend sufficient time in France to supervise the work yourself, they will do this, too, on your behalf.

When you have found the property you wish to buy, you will be asked to sign a preliminary contract, which will commit you and the vendor to complete the deal, subject to certain conditions. You may prefer not to sign there and then, but to return home to study the contract at your relative leisure and take advice on it. The language used in legal documents is very different from the French you will read in newspapers, magazines, the latest best-seller or the menu in the restaurant. In seeking advice, however, you will need rather more than a simple translation of your documents. If you consult a legal professional in Britain, choose someone who is well-versed in French law, conveyancing and tax considerations, and who is qualified to go through the paperwork with you thoroughly , explaining all its implications. What has been left out of your contract can be just as important as its contents.

Do not commit yourself until you understand fully what you are signing. It is all too easy to become involved in the wonderful ambiance of France, to fall in love with a house and to sign a contract and pay a deposit without having thought very carefully about what you are doing. In fact, you will be committing yourself to buying the property and, if you change your mind, you will very likely lose the money you have paid.

Do take independent, professional advice, therefore, if you are in doubt about anything. Prepare thoroughly, and be sure you really have found the house you want. Think about how easy or difficult it will be to sell the house at a future date. Is it the sort of property that will interest a French buyer? Ask yourself if you are structuring your purchase in the right way. What about the tax implications? What about French inheritance law? Take your time. There is no harm in spending a few days, rather than a few hours or even just a few minutes, thinking things over. House-hunting in France will be fun. Enjoy it. Enjoy, too, the delicious prospect of having that place of your own in a magnificent country but, at the same time, do all you can to ensure that the reality will match the dream.

Chapter 3
Value for Money

TOM ROWLAND
Tom Rowland is the Property Correspondent of *The Daily Telegraph* and *The Sunday Telegraph*

Comparisons are invidious, but it is not hard to see why the scramble for houses in France has maintained momentum during a period when the property market in Britain has experienced a dramatic fall.

A single example with a deliberately rural tone illustrates the point. Yonder Marsh Farm is the sort of country retreat nestling in a crook on a Devon hillside which was a snip in 1979 when Strutt and Parker, the estate agent who handled its recent sale, estimate it would have gone for around £50,000. This year it was on the market with what was sourly described as a 'realistic' asking price of £250,000.

While the purchasers got an undeniably pleasant and well-restored cottage with a spectacular view, a few acres of ground, four bedrooms and a cider press, much the same sort of thing could be had in France for less than £50,000. A timber-framed farmhouse of around the same size in wooded grounds with unimpeded views over the Loire valley was for sale at the same time not far from Angers. The local agent, Avis Immobilier Angers, was asking £44,000.

The bulk of the interest in French property since 1988 has been in country cottage-type establishments, and by crossing the Channel buyers can bypass the huge inflation in property prices that has occurred in the most popular areas of Britain over the last decade.

One of the ironies of the market for country property in Britain in the late 1980s was that as increasing numbers of people decided they would like holiday cottages, fewer and fewer could actually afford the entry prices – which by the end of the decade were commonly quoted in parts of a million. As it is still possible to buy tumbledown houses in out-of-the-way parts of the French countryside for virtually the same price as a year's subscription to a glossy magazine, and the Channel Tunnel and the motorway network being built in France are about to improve communications significantly, it is hardly surprising that the countryside

in France has become something of a fashion product over here.

That is not to say that it is realistic to expect the kind of price rises in the coming decade which characterised the market in areas like Devon over the past ten years.

There are, however, pockets where prices have rocketed - principally places near the coast - and British buyers fortunate enough to have bought in these areas experienced in 1989 and the first half of 1990 the kind of house price boom that we saw back home in 1988.

Supplementary costs of purchase

The supplementary costs of buying a house in France are much higher than in Britain, with the notary's and estate agent's fees between them amounting to something like 20 per cent of the final sale price for a small to medium-sized property. So with prices historically rising at only 4 or 5 per cent per year for as far back as anybody cares to remember in many areas, this means that a house must be kept for a minimum of five years before its sale will show a profit on the transaction charges alone.

Mortgages are much cheaper in France, with interest rates of around 10 per cent, although repaying in French francs became progressively more expensive with the fall in the relative value of sterling in 1990.

There seems to be a psychological cut-off point for many buyers from the UK, who are unwilling to pay out over £50,000 to £70,000 for a property which they intend to use only a few weeks a year on holiday. Outside the obvious areas where prices are likely to continue booming it is worth remembering this when it comes to restoration and building works, because getting back much of the money spent on an expensive restoration could prove difficult and will inevitably involve waiting for a buyer prepared to pay some kind of premium. In places like the Pas de Calais the market is, in any case, exclusively British. The French neither want what they regard as isolated shacks in the cooler regions of the country, nor can they understand those who look on them as forgotten treasures.

The motorway effect

As the motorway network grows, increasing numbers of commuters may be tempted to villages with exceptionally good communications to a big town, but without a dramatic change in national attitudes there is not going to be a large indigenous demand for many years for the country houses the British drool over.

Those who buy ought to remember that they are buying part of a plentiful resource which is not particularly valued by the local middle classes and which the system has ensured they cannot make quick profits from dealing in. The exceptions are the pockets of expansion – to be accurate pockets and sleeves, because along the side of the motorways the French countryside is starting to experience something akin to the so-called 'M4 effect', with villages and towns nearest to the junctions becoming more prized than those closer in but without a fast route out. If the pattern holds, it will lead to corridors of prosperity.

There is a great deal of road-building underway or planned in France, and by the end of the century the motorway system will be greatly extended. There is bound to be a knock-on effect of the high prices of houses around Calais as British families find that more and more of the surrounding countryside is within commuting distance of Britain. But the peculiarity of the Calais property market could also be extended, with resales likely to be to other people from Britain. Around Calais the links with the UK are strong enough to have prompted a marked slow-down in the property market, mirroring conditions over the Channel.

Further away from the port it is sometimes hard to be sure where the exact route of the new roads will be. As we have seen, in contrast to Britain the local searches carried out by a French notary prior to the purchase of a French property do not include information about any major roads that may be planned or under construction in the vicinity of the property. The planning certificate (*certificat d'urbanisme*) that is issued by the local planning office only makes reference to public works that touch the property directly. It is worth checking to ensure that your dream holiday home will not be 100 yards from six lanes of roaring traffic in a few months' time, but if you are lucky enough to be in the corridor of a new road without its disturbing the tranquillity of the immediate surroundings, then the investment potential is considerable.

A motorway link from Calais to Rouen via Abbeville is the most immediate prospect for improved journey times to a port of entry from Britain, but much of Normandy, Brittany, the Loire valley and the Charente will be opened up to very quick access over the next few years, and properties close to these routes must have added attractions for British buyers. France is, after all, an enormous country, and, unlike Spain, it is almost all habitable, with potentially charming places to live in abundance. The peripheries, including the areas closest to visiting Britons, also suffer from chronic rural depopulation, and this, combined with inheritance laws that divide estates strictly among all of the offspring, means that there is a constant ready supply of properties for sale.

High-priced areas

The boundaries of the high-priced pockets where prices have shot ahead

BARBERS
Estate Agents
HAND PICKED PROPERTIES
IN RURAL TRANQUILITY

can be a little on the elastic side, according to a new report from Les Clos de France, an independent relocation agent based in Richmond. It goes on to say that 'Some property developers market their properties using the name of a famous resort when their properties are in fact on the outskirts, often in a different district with less prestige and fewer prospects.' Some properties which the sellers claim to be in Saint Tropez are in fact an hour's drive from the famous Place des Lices at its centre.

The report looks at 56 resort areas, from sizzling Cannes on the Côte d'Azur, via the Normandy port of Honfleur, much admired by Britons with a taste for eight-storey timber-framing and drizzle, to the muddy shores of the Ile de Noirmoutier, which juts out into the Bay of Biscay. It tips six for future growth: Le Touquet, Deauville, La Baule, the Saint Tropez bay, Cannes and Antibes. The last is reportedly undergoing a vast transformation with the development of the biggest property project on the Côte d'Azur, Antibes-Les-Pins, which is in part designed to accommodate some of the computer and software specialists who have come to the area between Grasse and Valbonne. It will eventually have 1400 flats, but the influx of high technology employers has created an accommodation squeeze which inevitably continues to push prices up in an area whose economy seems increasingly to resemble a piece of the California sun belt.

Prices are also extremely high in La Baule, the watering hole on the south Brittany coast which was all faded glory and family holidays a few years ago. The town is now experiencing a rebirth with smart tennis, golf and sporting complexes attracting younger and better-off holidaymakers, and a new three-hour rail link to Paris, courtesy of the TGV high-speed train.

The TGV is also expected shortly at Deauville, putting it an hour and a half's journey away from Paris. A building programme is well underway to improve many of the town's facilities, although the now slightly shabby *Belle Epoque* villas are slowly disappearing in the process, and, sadly, nobody seems very keen on preserving them.

Finding the high-growth pockets may well be a game many will try to play. Agents tip the area around Nantes because high demand from new employers is combining with that from second home-owners to create a shortage. Coastal areas in the south are bound to see high prices too, as the French continue to use this as their prime holiday ground. But most of provincial France will continue to be a happy hunting ground for those in search of the kind of country retreat they could only dream of owning back in Britain.

Local resistance to foreign buyers

There can be very different problems for the unwary in other towns not so used to influxes of outsiders keen to buy up the local heritage. The wave of British bargain-hunters buying holiday homes in Honfleur ran into a spot of local opposition in 1989, in the form of protests by the local major and council. Of the 65 houses and apartments sold in the centre of the town in the 18 months to the end of 1989, 25 went to British buyers, and the mayor, M Marcel Liabastre, and his deputy, Councillor Henri Lecheray, decided that it was possible to have too much of a good thing. The mayor announced that he was going to use discretionary powers under the town planning regulations to block sales to what he regarded as British speculators. Although, as M Lacheray pointed out, the town was not the only one along the coast to have had enough, no other has so far followed suit and attempted to ban British buyers.

The centre of Honfleur was designated a conservation zone in the early 1970s and all transactions involving its 1800 homes have to be reported to the town council. The mayor has discretionary powers to intervene in a sale and can insist that any property be sold to the council at a rate fixed to exclude 'speculative' gain. A vendor can refuse a sale but the property cannot be returned to the open market for four years. 'It is not that we have anything against the English – we are more than happy to see them. But some have started to speculate in property in the centre of the old town,' M Lacheray complained.

Prices of the narrow, seven- and eight-storey fishermen's houses which surround the old harbour in the centre of Honfleur have shot up, spurred by British demand, and local passions were aroused by a story of one Englishman who reputedly bought a house for FF300,000 and sold it a year later for FF600,000.

M Lacheray declared: 'If people want to buy houses away from the centre of the town or in the country, that is fine. But too many holiday homes will kill the commercial centre.

'Ten years ago we had to fight to keep the Parisians out, but the pressure from the British is far more severe.'

Advantages for the British – and the French

Honfleur is on the south bank of the Seine estuary and within easy reach of the ferry ports at Le Havre and Caen. Its cobbled streets, lined with tall, timber-framed buildings, have proved immensely popular with the new wave of British buyer, keen to pick up a cheap holiday home. When I was in the town to report on events in the town hall, a roadside advertisement on the way out of Honfleur announced '*Fruits, vins, vieux Calvados, cidre, fromages, miel.*' The Volvo and Nissan outside the shop, 300 metres further on, both sported British registrations, and the owners had the air of regular supermarket shoppers rather than passing motorists.

The scene encapsulated both the attractions that this part of France offers British visitors and the dilemma faced by the locals. The north is depressed, and for years there has been no queue to live in its draughty old houses. Now communications are about to improve dramatically, with a new bridge over the Seine which will eventually cut journeys from Honfleur to the ferry ports to just a few minutes. The biggest price rises could be yet to come.

A sign in the window of one of the half-dozen estate agents to be found in the old quarter of Honfleur read: '*Ancienne maison Normande restaurée. Vue splendide.*' You do not need to be a linguist to work out what was for sale, and just to help there was a picture of a half-timbered thatched house with a view down yet another lightly wooded valley. The photograph could have been from one of those lush remote corners of Surrey but the difference was in the price. Instead of the £300,000 such a property would cost around Guildford or Godalming, or the £150,000 you would pay further west, the asking price was just over £50,000. However, there is likely to be a substantial rise in prices before 1992 is just a dim memory.

But how much do those living in many of the most charming houses really want to sell, and how far can their asking prices be beaten down? An example in Brittany highlights many of the issues, from the other side.

Nadine Clermont is 24, unemployed and, in common with many of her age in rural France, prefers to help on the farm rather than face the alternative of working in a big city. Her brother Alain is a year younger. His hold on the world of work is only made possible at all because of the continuing generosity of the Common Agricultural Policy towards small farmers such as his father, whom he also helps on the farm. The course of both their lives is being changed, not through restructuring of the EC agricultural policy, but because of the effect the surge of British housebuyers is having on the area within striking distance of the St Malo ferry.

Louis Clermont, his wife Marie and the four youngest of their six children live with Marie's parents in a sixteenth-century manor on the edge of the Forêt de St Aubin between Lamballe and the beautiful craggy coast, not far from St Malo on the Côtes du Nord. Last summer they put the Manoir La Hessardais with about four acres on the market for a million francs, roughly £100,000. It was towards the British that the family was looking for a buyer. After years of stagnation caused by the

VIVE LA FRANCE

MAKE THE FRENCH CONNECTION

From cottages to chateaux, from weekend retreats to permanent homes, Farrar Stead & Glyn have the answer.
With 10 years' experience of the French property market and with knowledgeable regional representatives living in France, we have built up an impressive portfolio of properties.

Charming thatched colombage pressoir, 8kms from Honfleur. Very comfortable property, full of character, set in the most delightful countryside bordered by woods and fields.

FARRAR STEAD & GLYN

When "en route" for France make sure you call at Farrar Stead & Glyn !

071-731 4391

HORNER HILL INTERNATIONAL

WICKHAM FARM, HAYWARDS HEATH,
WEST SUSSEX RH16 1UL
Tel: (0444) 416733 Fax: (0444) 414006

A COMPLETE SERVICE FOR THE SALE AND PURCHASE OF PROPERTY IN FRANCE

SPECIALISTS IN RESIDENTIAL, COMMERCIAL AND INVESTMENT PROPERTY

General research and property search
Assistance in negotiation of purchases
Assistance in arranging finance
Engagement of a Notaire
Provision of a tax advisory service through an accredited firm
Organisation of property surveys
Feasibility studies
Organisation of project design team and architects
Engagement of an international removal firm if required

FULL CONSULTANCY SERVICE OFFERED ON THE BASIS OF A REFUNDABLE RETAINER

PICARDY

For our selection of properties within one hour's drive of the channel tunnel contact:

County Estate Agencies (France) Ltd.

32 Bouverie Square, Folkestone CT20 1BA
Tel: 0303 221077 Fax: 0303 44409

system and the remoteness of the region from the high-tech boom of modern France, prices are on the move, spurred in this case by purchasers who find the lure of a *château* in a rural idyll for the price of a suburban semi in the south of England hard to resist.

But while stories abound in the local cafés around Lamballe of overseas buyers prepared to pay well over the odds for ruins nobody wants, it is still very much a buyer's market, with a surplus of old buildings. Good cottages go locally for about £25,000 upwards.

'If we can get a good price my parents would like to build a new house near here so that my brother could go on farming the rest of the land,' says Nadine. 'I would like to stay here, but my father says it is going to cost almost as much to repair the old parts of this house as it would to build a new one. He is keen to move. He argues with my grandfather, who would like to stay, but then he is old and ill.'

Jean Morand, the grandfather, came to La Hessardais in 1934 and farmed the place continuously, if not very profitably. After a lifetime of being bossed about by his father-in-law, it is not hard to see why M Clermont Snr would like to find somewhere else to live.

In common with many old houses in the French countryside, the manor is a mixture of slightly botched repair and neglect; the ground floor of the main house is now used for the production of cider and Calvados, and the first floor is a series of grain stores. Only the wing which makes up one side of the central courtyard is used for living space, so there is much scope for that key element in the romantic castle-owning syndrome, restoration and rebuilding of the undervalued and decayed.

Unlike the structure of many of the tumbledown barns in this part of France, the thick stone walls of the manor seem sturdy enough, though they were built in the first place as bastions of the *ancien régime*. The manor was put up as Henry IV consolidated his grip on France and needed all the help he could get from a hierarchical rural society to keep the lid on brewing rebellion. Later in the nineteenth century, it suffered like the rest of France from a neglect of the countryside. The Côtes du Nord was one of the poorest *départements*, and there are significantly fewer big houses here than almost anywhere north of the threadbare parts of the Massif Central. Even in these more prosperous times, few of the houses have been well maintained. In the case of La Hessardais, part of the roof blew off during the gales in October 1987 and has yet to be replaced.

The countryside is still somewhere from which the people who live there yearn to escape, even if they do not quite have the courage to do it.

'This house is a bit of a problem really. I think I would prefer something new and near my friends,' says Alain. His sister adds: 'If we leave, perhaps I will find a job and a life in the town, but it will be a foreigner who buys.'

And she is probably right. French suburbanites generally go for holiday homes by the sea, preferably the Mediterranean, and inland it is foreigners who act as catalysts for rural change.

Buyer beware

Finding property in France is not complicated, and most people can manage to find something suitable on their own. However, an agent in Britain can save time because French estate agents still have a poor reputation for marketing and presentation. For the right price, the manor with its tower and pretty setting will make a magnificent home for someone with the time and resources to do the restoration properly, but elsewhere 'Buy in haste and repent at leisure' could well be the motto to apply to some kinds of French property. It is possible to end up with a pretty white elephant which consumes resources for little return and is difficult to sell.

The actor John Hurt, famous for such films as *Scandal* and *The Elephant Man*, put his house in Brittany up for sale in the spring of 1990. It was tucked away in one of the fat portfolios of country cottages offered by Brittany agent Philippe Guégan from Pontivy, one of the exhibitors at the *Daily Telegraph* French Property Event at Olympia. According to M Guégan: 'Mr Hurt bought it last year, but I think it was a bit of a fantasy, and he decided he did not really want the house soon after paying for it.' Apparently, Mr Hurt had bought a house elsewhere in France and no longer needed one in Brittany.

The slate-roofed, stone-walled farm on two floors is close to Mur-de-Bretagne, in the centre of the Brittany peninsula, about as far from the sea as it is possible to get. The building has five large rooms and was on the market partly renovated. The price came down from around £50,000 to £40,000, and the actor was open to an even lower offer. He was reluctant to talk about the extent to which he felt bruised by the property transaction, but his experience seems to show that buying pleasant, run-down houses is not necessarily all fun. Getting the money out again can be difficult, if only because the French are so stubbornly uninterested in the cottages.

Are improvements worthwhile?

Those people buying in the countryside will have to undertake home improvements of one kind or another: the trick is to know how much

BLACK DIAMONDS

Truffles make the ladies and the gentlemen gallant.

Brillat Savarin

The truffle is a fungus - *Tuber Melanosporum* - black in colour and ranging in size from something no larger than an acorn to an object as big as one's fist and weighing perhaps half a kilo. Its surface is rough and convoluted and the fleshy interior is veined like marble, containing within it the minute spores from which the fungus develops. It grows on the roots of oaks, just below the surface of the earth, and the presence of truffles is usually indicated by a ring of 'burnt ground' which appears in the autumn above the place where lhe truffle will be found. If the truffle is very close to the surface its precise location within the ring may be revealed by a slight swelling and cracking of the soil just above it. Otherwise it has to be detected by other means and the time-honoured method is to employ a sow on some kind of lead. The sow has a natural taste for truffles and will find them from their aroma and by feeling the ground with its snout. The truffles can then be dug out with a metal-pointed tool. Dogs can also be trained to sniff them out and have the advantage of moving around faster, especially where there is brushwood or fallen branches lying about. On a calm winter's day a column of tiny, yellow flies will hover above a truffle leading, it is said, the skilled truffle-hunter to the spot where one may be found. He will mark it, taking care not to disturb the flies too much in case they settle over several places. How many hours must have been spent by amateurs looking for columns of yellow flies! For the expert there are many false alarms; equally, stories of surprise discoveries are legion. They are all part of the mystery and legend that has come to surround this curious object.

For the lowdown on PROPERTY, consult the experts - we're bilingual - PERIGORD WEEKEND, phone (010 33) 53 55 06 32 or Fax 53 55 20 95, or 14 rue Jean-Jaures, 24800 Thiviers, Dordogne, France for a Free Catalogue.

Text reproduced by kind permission of David & Charles Publishers, Newton Abbot, from *The Dordogne Region in France* by Ian Scargill, published 1974. Illustration reproduced by kind permission of M.D. Gibert, 2400 Thiviers, France.

The evolution of motorway construction in France

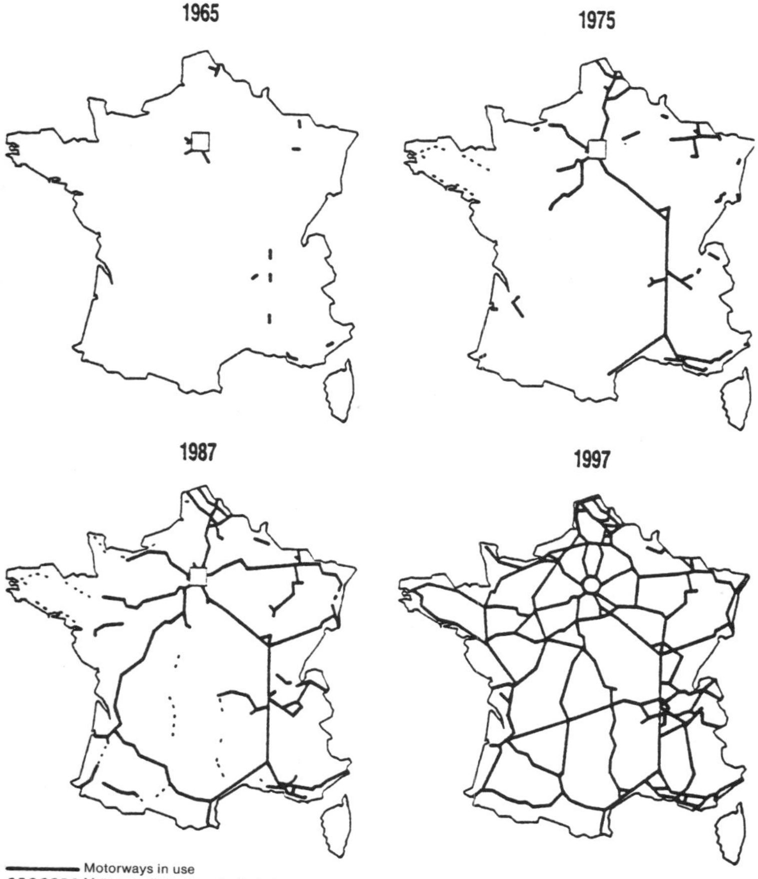

Motorways in use
Motorway links (eventually to become motorways)

Ministère de l'Equipement, du Logement, de l'Aménagement du Territoire et des Transports

work is worthwhile, and when to stop. If you are going to keep a property for many years, there is no reason for not restoring it to the point at which you are happy with the end product; but bear in mind that after a point soon reached, this will be money spent for enjoyment and not an investment one can realistically expect to recoup.

The classic example must be the farmhouse which has been virtually untouched since the nineteenth century. There would be no modern kitchen, bathroom or lavatory, the roof would certainly need urgent repair, and if there is a damp course it will need reinforcing.

Some people bring building materials, workmen and hired help from home and try to have as little to do with the local tradesmen as possible. While it is easier to control quality in this way, there are drawbacks (see Chapter 9), and apart from not being the best way of ingratiating yourself with the locals, you will not be able to claim the costs against either capital gains tax (33 per cent) or any income made from renting.

For most people the problems of investment in a French property should be small compared with the fun to be had. The wine is cheap, the food magnificent, and the time it takes to get there can only shrink in the next few years.

The French real estate market in 1989

Regional averages

(By courtesy of *L'Observateur de l'Immobilier* and Crédit Foncier de France)

	Three-bedroom houses New or old in good condition	 Old, needing renovation
ALSACE Strasbourg Mulhouse	F 750–800,000	F 450–500,000
AQUITAINE Bordeaux Pau	F 500–900,000	F 300–400,000
AUVERGNE Clermont-Ferrand Moulins	F 500–600,000	F 200–300,000

	Three-bedroom houses	
	New or old in good condition	Old, needing renovation
BASSE-NORMANDIE Caen	F 600,000	F 400,000
BOURGOGNE Dijon, Mâcon Auxerre	F 450–600,000	F 200–420,000
BRETAGNE Rennes, Brest Vannes	F 400–650,000	F 200–420,000
CENTRE Orléans Tours, Chartres	F 500–1,000,000	F 250–500,000
CHAMPAGNE-ARDENNES Reims Troyes	F 600–800,000	F 300–400,000
FRANCHE-COMTE Besançon Belfort	F 500–600,000	F 350–380,000
HAUTE-NORMANDE Rouen, Evreux Le Hâvre	F 650–700,000	F 400,000
LANGUEDOC-ROUSSILLON Montpellier Nîmes, Perpignan	F 900,000	F 320–450,000
LIMOUSIN Limoges, Brive	F 550–600,000	F 300,000
LOIRE Angers, Laval Le Mans, Nantes	F 500–600,000	F 200–300,000

	Three-bedroom houses New or old in good condition	Old, needing renovation
LORRAINE Nancy, Metz	F 700–730,000	F 420–450,000
MIDI-PYRENEES Toulouse	F 800,000	F 400,000
NORD-PAS DE CALAIS Lille, Arras	F 450–500,000	F 200–250,000
PICARDIE Amiens, Beauvais Compiègne	F 600–650,000	F 180–400,000
POITOU-CHARENTES Poitiers Angoulême La Rochelle	F 500–550,000	F 300–350,000
PROVENCE-ALPES COTE D'AZUR Marseille, Nice, Avignon, Aix/Provence, Toulon	F1,200–1,800,000	F 500–1,500,000
RHONE-ALPES Chambéry, Lyon, Grenoble, St-Etienne, Annecy, Valence	F 650–1,600,000	F 300–700,000
YVELINES Versailles Rambouillet	F 780–1,600,000	F 500–1,100,000

Chapter 4

Contracts and Conveyancing

MALCOLM KEOGH
Malcolm Keogh is a partner in the international firm of solicitors, Pannone Blackburn, and an *agent consulaire de France*.

Introduction

Many readers will be more or less familiar with the various steps involved in buying a house in England and Wales. The transaction takes place in two main stages. There is a preliminary contract and, some weeks later, the transaction is completed by the signing of a deed of sale. In France too, the purchase of property involves two stages. As in England, there is a preliminary contract which is followed some weeks later by the signature of a deed (*l'acte de vente*) whereby ownership of the property is transferred to the purchaser. Here, however, the similarity between the two systems ends. French law, unlike English law, has its origins in Roman law and is codified in *le Code Civil* which first came into being at the beginning of the nineteenth century. Readers should not therefore fall into the trap of believing that because they are reasonably familiar with English procedures, the French procedure may be accepted at face value without enquiry. In this chapter we explain the main differences between the two systems and highlight the areas where the British purchaser should take particular care to ensure that his interests are fully protected.

The various stages of a purchase

The first stage in the transaction is the preliminary contract, which is followed some weeks later by the signing of the deed of sale, whereby the ownership of the property is passed from vendor to purchaser. While in England a contract for the sale of land must be in writing, there is no such requirement in French law. In theory at least, a verbal agreement for the sale and purchase of a house could be binding, although it is rare in practice. It is worth noting that an enforceable agreement may be made inadvertently by exchange of correspondence with the vendor, the estate agent or the *notaire*. Normally, however, there is a preliminary contract which may take a number of forms. There is no universal form of contract so the purchaser must ensure that he understands the document offered to him and that it contains all the appropriate clauses for his protection. There are a number of different types of preliminary contract and the type of contract varies depending upon whether you are buying an existing property or a new property in the course of construction or recently built.

Contracts used for the sale and purchase of existing property

There are three main types of contract in use for the sale and purchase of existing property: the *promesse de vente*, the *promesse d'achat* and the *vente sous conditions suspensives* (also known as the *compromis de vente*). The main distinction between these different kinds of contract is that the first two consist of a unilateral engagement (by the vendor or the purchaser, respectively), whereas the third type is a bilateral contract where both parties are bound to the transaction. All three types of contract will include what are known as *conditions suspensives*, the effect of which is to make the contract conditional upon the happening of certain events. We shall look at *conditions suspensives* in more detail later in this chapter.

The *promesse de vente*

The *promesse de vente* is a unilateral promise by the vendor to sell the property to the purchaser at a certain price. Thus, the purchaser is granted an option to buy. This option may be for a specified period within which the purchaser must inform the vendor of his intention to buy. The vendor may not withdraw from the contract until the agreed time has elapsed. Alternatively, there may be no specified period and the vendor may withdraw from the sale at any time prior to the acceptance of the option by the purchaser. This contract will normally include strict provisions regarding the option and the purchaser must carefully observe those provisions, otherwise he may lose his rights altogether.

In many ways, the *promesse de vente* is unsatisfactory to both vendor and purchaser. The vendor does not have any great certainty that the purchaser will opt to buy and the purchaser may also be at risk if the contract permits the vendor to withdraw. Furthermore, a purchaser would be faced with complex legal difficulties (and interminable delays) if the vendor should die before the option is taken, or if any action should be taken against the vendor by a creditor with a mortgage over the property. Despite these drawbacks, this type of contract is popular in certain parts of France.

This unilateral promise to sell made by the vendor permits the potential purchaser to consider the purchase in a relatively leisurely way without having a firm obligation to go ahead with the purchase. However, if the purchaser decides eventually not to proceed he will normally be required to indemnify the vendor for the loss which he sustains because of his inability to sell the property to anybody else in the intervening period. Normally, a *promesse de vente* requires the purchaser to complete the purchase within a specified time and if the purchaser does not do so the vendor is then free to offer the property again on the market.

From the point of view of the purchaser it is important to note that, although there is no *obligation* upon the purchaser to proceed, this type of contract normally contains a stipulation that, if the purchaser does not proceed, the amount of a deposit paid will be forfeit and retained by the vendor in lieu of damages for what in French is called the *immobilisation* of the property during the existence of the option granted by the contract. On the other hand, the purchaser may formally take up the option, or declare his intention to purchase, in which case the *promesse de vente* will be regarded as having been perfected. The *promesse de vente* is generally considered by *notaires* to be the kind of contract most favourable to the purchaser as it allows the purchaser considerable flexibility.

The *promesse d'achat*

More rarely encountered than the *promesse de vente*, the *promesse d'achat* is again a unilateral contract, but here the purchaser commits himself to purchase the property in the event that the vendor subsequently agrees to sell it. Thus, an option is granted to the purchaser to buy the property, but there is no *obligation* upon the vendor to sell it at all. In this sense it is the reverse of the *promesse de vente*. Again, it is essential that the option is granted only for a limited time and upon the expiration of the time specified the contract becomes null and void. This type of contract, which is the least favourable to the purchaser, is unfortunately becoming more common and it is essential for the potential purchaser not to enter into such a contract without clearly understanding its implications. In particular, the time limit as specified in the contract should be as short as possible as the purchaser remains potentially bound to purchase if the vendor should choose to sell before the time limit specified. However, as in the case of the *promesse de vente*, the purchaser may have the right to refuse to proceed with the purchase when the vendor requires him to do so, but on condition that the purchaser would then lose the deposit paid.

The *vente sous conditions suspensives* or *compromis de vente*

This kind of contract is in many ways similar to a preliminary contract for the sale and purchase of property in England in that it is *bilateral* in nature as it binds *both* parties to the transaction. The contract not only specifies the property but also the price agreed to be paid and provides for payment of a deposit upon the signing of the contract - usually 10 per cent of the purchase price. Again, this contract will invariably contain *conditions suspensives* (see page 58), all of which must be satisfied before the contract can be regarded as 'perfect'. Once the conditions have been satisfied, the parties are required to proceed to the next stage - the signing of the *acte de vente* or conveyance deed. Thus, in this case, the purchaser has no right to abandon the transaction, even upon loss of his deposit, unless the contract specifically permits him to do so on that basis.

Contracts used for the sale and purchase of new property

As in the case of existing properties, there are many different forms of contract generally in use for the sale of new properties. They can, however, generally be divided into three main categories: the *contrat de réservation*, the *vente en l'état futur d'achèvement* and the *vente à terme*.

The *contrat de réservation*

The so-called *contrat de réservation* is neither a *promesse de vente* nor an option, but is a separate kind of contract in its own right. In exchange for the payment of a deposit, the vendor undertakes to reserve for the purchaser a particular building or part of a building. Unlike a contract for the sale of an existing property, a *contrat de réservation* must include a detailed description of the building, including the specifications and quality of materials to be used and the dates by which the construction of each stage of the building must be completed, as well as the price to be paid by the purchaser. The deposit must be paid into a separate bank account and may not be paid to the developer until the completion of the transaction. Furthermore, the deposit cannot be seized from that bank account in the event, for example, of the developer's bankruptcy or liquidation because it is deemed not to belong to the developer until completion. The law provides clear protection for the purchaser so that the deposit must be returned if, for example, completion does not take place through the fault of the vendor or if, for example, the building does not meet the specification contained in the contract. The French courts have on numerous occasions been called upon to interpret the many different forms of *contrat de réservation* which exist, and such contracts have on occasions been considered as the equivalent of a *promesse de vente* (so that the developer is obliged to complete the transaction), while on other occasions they have been regarded as nothing more than a reservation of the building for the purchaser *if* the vendor subsequently chooses to sell it. If the vendor decides not to proceed, the purchaser would be entitled to the return of his deposit, but whether or not he would be entitled to any other compensation would depend upon the individual contract. The *contrat de réservation* is followed by a deed of sale (*acte de vente*), a draft of which must be sent to the purchaser at least one month before the date of completion.

The *vente en l'état futur d'achèvement*

Unlike the *contrat de réservation*, which merely reserves the building for the purchaser who only acquires ownership later, once the building has been completed, a contract known as a *vente en l'état futur d'achèvement* provides that the vendor will build a building but will sell it to the purchaser before the construction has been completed. A purchaser enjoys certain legal protections, provided that the property is intended for use as a dwelling or for mixed use such as dwelling and business, and provided that the contract requires the purchaser to make payments on account before the completion of the building work. In this case, the contract must conform with the Civil Code, which requires the vendor to transfer to the purchaser at the outset the ownership of the land and of the building insofar as it is built. The rest of the building becomes the property of the purchaser as and when it is built and the purchaser is required to make payments in accordance with the progress of the building works.

The *vente à terme*

The Civil Code permits a third kind of contract, the *vente à terme*, which is a contract whereby the vendor undertakes to transfer the building to the purchaser and the purchaser undertakes to take delivery and to pay the purchase price on completion of the building work. The subsequent deed declares that the building works have been completed.

If the property is one of a type where the purchaser enjoys protection under *le Code Civil* (see above), both the *vente en l'état futur d'achèvement* and the *vente à terme* must be signed before a *notaire* or by *procuration* (power of attorney – see page 61). Furthermore, both types of contract must contain certain obligatory terms. Failure to do so could result in the contract being declared null and void.

Beware of the so-called 'commercial contract' or '*parahotel*', which has the effect of avoiding important consumer protection legislation which requires builders to enter into bank guarantees to ensure the completion of the property in the event of the builder's bankruptcy, etc. The use of this kind of contract may be very prejudicial to the purchaser.

Whether the contract used is a *contrat de réservation*, a *vente en l'état futur d'achèvement* or a *vente à terme*, all contain *conditions suspensives*. Each type of contract provides for payment of a deposit and stage payments.

Signing the preliminary contract

Whereas in England a preliminary contract will normally be drawn up by a solicitor or other qualified person by reference to the vendor's title deeds or registration details, this will not necessarily be the case in France. Unless you have agreed directly with the owner of the property or a *notaire* has negotiated the sale (see Chapter 2), it will probably be an estate agent who prepares the preliminary contract. Each agent has his favourite form and once a purchaser has been found and a price agreed, the estate agent will simply fill in the details of vendor and purchaser, add the details of the property and ask the purchaser to sign the contract and pay a deposit – usually 10 per cent of the purchase price. Note, however, that it is essential that the contract, once signed, is passed to the *notaire* who must record its details. If this does not happen, the contract may not be enforceable later.

Although the estate agent may bring pressure to bear, suggesting that the price may increase or that there are other purchasers waiting to sign a contract, it is unwise to enter into a commitment hastily. A purchaser should allow himself time to consider the transaction, understand the full terms of the contract offered and, if appropriate, negotiate the inclusion of additional *conditions suspensives* to protect his interests (see page 58). Remember also that the fact that an estate agent inserts the name of the vendor and details of the property does not necessarily prove that the vendor owns the property! If the estate agent seems unwilling to allow you, say, a fortnight to consider the contract or take advice, he may be prepared to do so upon payment of a nominal non-returnable 'good-faith' deposit. While not legally binding, an arrangement of this kind can sometimes provide the time needed to ensure that the contract contains nothing detrimental.

Conditions suspensives

Certain conditions, the *conditions suspensives*, are common to all kinds of contract, whether for the sale of existing property or new property. The existence of these *conditions suspensives* is another major difference between the English and the French systems of buying and selling property. Readers may recall that when buying a property in England and Wales, the solicitor acting for the purchaser will always advise that the preliminary contract should not be signed until the result of a search with the local authority has been received and reveals nothing detrimental, and until the purchaser has not only arranged his finance but actually received a written offer of finance from his bank or building society. Quite the reverse is true in France.

The preliminary contract (in whatever form it may be) is signed first of all, but is held to be *conditional* upon certain important matters. With the exception of the condition relating to finance (see page 59) these conditions are *not* obligatory and the purchaser should therefore take care to ensure that all necessary conditions are included in the contract which is offered to him. These special conditions are called in French *conditions suspensives* – ie the contract is 'suspended' until such time as all the conditions are fulfilled. If any one of them is not fulfilled, the contract would be regarded as null and void, as if it had never existed, and the purchaser is entitled to the return of his deposit. A purchaser should ensure that the contract is *at least* subject to the following conditions:

- that there are no planning proposals which might adversely affect the property;
- that there is no third-party right of way or easements which may adversely affect the purchaser's enjoyment of the property;
- that the vendor has not himself entered into any mortgage or charge over the property for a sum exceeding the selling price. This is particularly important as the French system of conveyancing and land registration gives no protection to a purchaser in this respect. If, after completion of the transaction, it was found that the vendor had mortgaged the property for a sum greater than the purchase price, the property would remain *charged* or mortgaged with the outstanding balance;
- that there are no third-party or State rights of pre-emption. This condition is particularly important in the case of country properties. In France, there exist State organisations known as *SAFER* (*Sociétés d'Aménagement Foncier et d'Etablissement Rural*) whose role is to supervise and ensure the economical utilisation of agricultural land. In many rural areas the *SAFER* has an overriding right to purchase a country

property whenever it comes up for sale. It is thus essential to obtain a certificate confirming that the *SAFER* does not intend to exercise that right.

If any one of these conditions is not satisfied, the contract is deemed to be null and void, and any deposit paid by the purchaser to the vendor will be returned, albeit without interest. It is always possible to negotiate additional *conditions suspensives*. For example, a purchaser of a house which is in questionable structural condition may insist upon a condition in the contract that the purchase is subject to a satisfactory survey. In practice, however, it is not usual in France for property to be surveyed prior to purchase and a vendor may well be reluctant to agree to the inclusion of such a clause.

While the various *conditions suspensives* mentioned above are not obligatory, there is one condition relating to the purchaser's financial arrangements which must be included, or at least referred to, whichever contract is used.

The *Loi Scrivener*

This law was passed by the French parliament on 13 July 1979, and named after the minister (Madame Christiane Scrivener) who promoted it. It is a major consumer protection measure, which lays down arrangements for the offer and acceptance of finance intended for house purchase as between the lender and the borrower. It also stipulates that a special *condition suspensive* must be included in every contract for the sale and purchase of property. This law, which only applies to private houses and to loans from financial institutions rather than informal loans (from family, friends, employer, etc), states that the preliminary contract must specify the intended amount of the loan. If the loan is refused, the contract will be deemed null and void and the deposit returned to the purchaser. If the purchaser does *not* intend to apply for a loan, the contract *must* be endorsed with a statement to that effect *in the handwriting of the purchaser.*

It will readily be seen that the existence of the condition in the contract required by *la Loi Scrivener* provides a major advantage over the English system. Whereas in England a purchaser runs the risk of losing the property to another purchaser or being 'gazumped' while he waits for the result of his mortgage application, in France he can effectively secure the property *before* the application for finance is made. However, great care must be exercised. The preliminary contract will not only contain details of the loan for which the purchaser intends to apply, but will also oblige the purchaser to make his application and provide the proposed lender with all necessary information within a certain time limit, often 15 days, after the signing of the contract. The buyer must notify the vendor immediately the loan application has been granted or refused. Failure to comply with the strict letter of the contract could result in the loss of the purchaser's right to withdraw without penalty, should this loan application be refused. For this reason, it is imperative that the purchaser should take care to ensure that the contract is dated with the date on which he actually signs. Do not, for example, sign a contract and return it to the vendor or his agent undated, as an earlier date may be inserted, such as the date on which the vendor himself signed the contract. Thus, the purchaser may be out of time for making his loan application even before he starts!

The deposit

A purchaser is normally required to pay a deposit of 10 per cent upon signing the preliminary contract, whatever kind of contract is used. Care should, however, be taken to understand the legal significance of this initial payment. It may be regarded under French law as either *les arrhes* or *un dédit*. *Les arrhes* are the equivalent of a deposit or payment on account to the vendor, and the purchaser may not withdraw from the contract simply on the basis that he will lose the deposit paid. The *dédit* on the other hand is more in the nature of a fixed penalty so that the purchaser may decline to proceed with the transaction in the knowledge that he will merely lose that deposit. Further, the sum paid on signing the initial contract may be referred to in a penal clause, so that it may then be forfeit not only if the purchaser does not proceed with the transaction, but even if he merely completes the transaction later than the date specified for completion. It is, therefore, extremely important for the purchaser to ascertain on what basis the deposit is being paid.

The deed of sale

If the property has been bought through an estate agent who has prepared the contract, the agent will, after signature of the contract, pass the file to the *notaire*, who deals with the transaction from then on. If no estate agent has been involved, the *notaire* himself will already have prepared the preliminary contract.

Having carried out his various enquiries, the *notaire* prepares the *acte de vente* or deed of sale. The *acte de vente* should follow the preliminary contract in its contents, but will deal with the description of the land more fully. This is the second stage of the transaction, and upon signature its effect is to transfer ownership from vendor to purchaser.

The role of the *notaire* is to authenticate documents signed in his presence. For this reason, the *acte de vente* is also often referred to as the *acte authentique*. In theory, therefore, it is necessary for both vendor and purchaser to attend in person at the office of the *notaire*, who reads the documents to them, witnesses their signatures and records the transaction. However, to avoid the inconvenience of having to travel to France merely to sign the documents, it is possible instead to make use of a *procuration*, or power of attorney.

The *procuration*

The *procuration*, or power of attorney, is a document drawn up in French and needs only to be signed before a notary public in the UK. Most towns have a solicitor who is also a notary public. When you have signed the procuration in his presence, the notary public forwards the document to the Foreign and Commonwealth Office, where a certificate known as the *Apostille* is endorsed. This validates the *procuration* for use by the French *notaire*. It may either appoint a friend of the purchaser to sign the deed on the purchaser's behalf or, more usually, it appoints a member of the *notaire*'s own staff.

Different *notaires* have different requirements so far as the *procuration* is concerned. However, if the deed of sale does not include a mortgage or charge in favour of a third party (a bank, etc), the *procuration* may not necessarily have to be signed in the presence of a notary public but may simply be signed by the purchaser and returned to the *notaire*. Some notaries, nevertheless, still require the document to be witnessed by a solicitor. Where there is a mortgage or charge over the property, the *procuration must* be signed before a notary public. Many French *notaires* still ask British purchasers to sign documents such as *procurations* before the nearest French Consul. This is, in fact, incorrect; French consulates no longer perform this function and the documents should be signed before a notary public.

However it is signed, the *acte de vente* is of crucial importance. Although it is subsequently registered or 'published' at the land registry, the contents of the *acte de vente* and in particular the description of the property conveyed take preference over the registration in the land registry. For this reason, the *notaire* is required to retain the original signed document, and the purchaser will not receive a bundle of title deeds or a land certificate as evidence of his ownership. If, therefore, you do require evidence of ownership – for example, for the purpose of importing personal furniture and effects into France free of VAT – you should ask the *notaire* at an early stage. He will provide you with either an *attestation*, which is a simple certificate that the transaction has been completed and that you are owner of the property, or alternatively an *expédition*, in which case the *notaire* will send you a certified copy of the deed of sale. Note, however, that you will receive neither unless you specifically ask!

The French 'scene'

The *notaire*

Although the *purchaser* always has the right to nominate a *notaire* to carry out the transaction, the British purchaser will often find he has little choice. As a matter of practice, an estate agent will usually suggest a particular *notaire* who will probably be the one who dealt with the previous sale of the property to the present vendor. Bear in mind, however, that you still have the choice of *notaire*, except where the property is new, or being sold 'on-plan', where the *notaire* appointed by the developer will deal with the transaction.

As we have seen in Chapter 2, once the file is in the hands of the *notaire* he will do a number of things. First, he will make the various enquiries with the local and departmental authorities on planning matters and obtain confirmation from the *SAFER* of non-exercise of the right of pre-emption, where appropriate. If he is not already familiar with the title, he will also check for any detrimental third-party rights or easements which may affect the property. Here again, we find a difference between the *notaire* and the English solicitor. While the British purchaser might seek progress reports and details of matters revealed by the local search from his solicitor, the *notaire* will not always volunteer such information. The French purchaser is generally quite happy to leave the matter in the *notaire*'s hands until the time comes for completion, or signature of the deed of sale.

It is important to note that the enquiries made by the *notaire* relate to the property itself, and not to the surrounding area. To be sure that nothing detrimental is planned for the immediate vicinity, the purchaser should examine the *plan d'occupation des sols* or 'plan of land occupancy', which is to be found at *La Direction Départementale de l'Equipement* for the *département* in which the property is situated. This shows the use to which the local area is dedicated. The *certificat d'urbanisme* can also provide valuable planning information, while the *cadastre* will show the precise area of land, by reference to a parcel number, which the purchaser intends to buy. Both can normally be found in the local *mairie* or town hall. The preliminary contract, whatever its form, should identify the land by reference to parcel numbers, which can easily be identified in the *cadastre*, and copies of local area plans may be obtained. The *cadastre* does not indicate ownership of each parcel of land, merely its extent. To ascertain ownership, a search needs to be made at the *Bureau des*

Hypothèques, which is normally found at departmental rather than local level.

In addition to the tasks described above, the *notaire* acting in the sale of new property will also prepare the *règlement de copropriété* or rules of co-ownership. This is generally a document of considerable length dealing with every aspect of the use of the property, and providing for the appointment of a *syndic*, or management company, and future payment of the purchaser's share of the maintenance of common parts of the building, roads, etc. It is common for these documents to be presented to the purchaser for signature with little or no explanation. There is no doubt that a purchaser would, under French law, be deemed to have agreed to all the terms of, for example, the *règlement de copropriété* even if he could show that he did not understand the document. It is, therefore, essential to obtain proper advice as to the contents of these documents before they are signed.

L'état civil

If you buy property in the UK, nobody is particularly concerned as to when and where you were born or your marital status. The French legal system looks at things in quite a different way. Before you can enter into any significant transaction in France you will be required to provide your *état civil* or civil status. Once the *notaire* receives the file relating to your purchase he will want you to supply him with the following information:

- your full names, maiden name (if applicable) and date and place of birth;
- your marital status and (if applicable) the date and place of marriage, or divorce;
- the *régime matrimonial* or 'matrimonial system' under which you were married. Under French law, a marriage may take place with or without a contract of marriage. Where the parties have entered into a contract of marriage, such contract may provide for joint ownership by the couple of all assets (*communauté des biens*) or separate ownership by each spouse of his or her own assets (*séparation des biens*). If there was no marriage contract, a couple will be deemed to have chosen the statutory régime of *communauté des biens*. A married woman is always referred to in French legal documents by her maiden name.

The *note de renseignements d'urbanisme*

The *note de renseignements d'urbanisme* may be likened to the local search certificate provided by local authorities in England. It sets out details of any administrative charges to which the property may be subject, such as planning or preservation orders which may have been made. It also sets out the permitted use of the land in question as well as any public rights of pre-emption.

The *certificat d'urbanisme*

The *certificat d'urbanisme* is necessary where land is being sold for the purpose of building. It should not be confused with the *autorisation de construire* which is in the nature of detailed planning permission. The *certificat d'urbanisme* is an administrative document which merely states whether or not a particular plot of land may be built upon.

Costs and expenses

The tax, stamp duty and notarial fees (all of which are collected by the *notaire*) are *always* paid by the purchaser, whereas estate agent's commission or the *notaire*'s commission for negotiating the sale where no estate agent was involved may be payable by the vendor or the purchaser depending on the custom in the region concerned.

The calculation of tax and stamp duty is extremely complex, and consists of a levy payable to the *département* as well as percentages payable in respect of local and regional taxes. To these are added land registry fees. Finally, the *notaire* is entitled to his own fee, calculated on a sliding scale which starts at 5 per cent and is reduced to less than 1 per cent for that part of the purchase price over FF 110,000. As a rule of thumb, it may be assumed that the purchaser of pre-owned property will have to pay a total of between 10 and 12 per cent of the purchase price in tax, stamp duty and notarial fees. However, the purchaser of a new property (which is defined as property built within the last five years and not having been sold during that time other than to a *marchand de biens*, or property dealer), enjoys a much lower total percentage of taxes and notarial fees. Here, the total will not exceed 3 to 4 per cent of the purchase price. However, in this case, French VAT (at the rate of 18.6 per cent at the time of writing) is *included* in the purchase price.

Chapter 5

Alternative Means of Ownership

FRANK RUTHERFORD
Frank Rutherford is senior partner of Rutherfords, French agents since 1963.

It always amuses me to tell my French friends that all land in Great Britain belongs to the Crown, and that any land we own is granted to us to hold freely in perpetuity. Although we may own the freehold, ultimate title still rests in the hands of our Monarch.

In a republic such as France these matters are much more cut and dried. You own your land and all that is constructed upon it and your title is guaranteed by the State. It is not even necessary to possess any title deeds to prove ownership, since the names of all property owners are recorded at the Land Registry. Every square metre of France has a number to it and each proprietor is duly listed.

With the passage of time, however, variations have developed and there are now a number of alternative ways of buying a French property.

Leasehold

Leasehold is a rare form of title. There are certain properties on which long leases have been granted (*baux emphytéotiques*) but these are uncommon and the average British purchaser is unlikely to come across them. Most conventional tenants have a lease, but unlike British practice, there is no intrinsic capital value to a lease allowing it to be bought or sold. Unless in protected tenancies, tenants pay the full rack rent. Only commercial leases change hands for a consideration, but again, values never reach the giddy heights achieved in this country.

Co-ownership

Most leasehold tenants in the United Kingdom occupy an apartment. This is because it is still impossible here to own the freehold of a flat (although a new system called commonhold is in the pipeline). In France, however, it is standard practice to own one's apartment outright and the system whereby this is done is called 'co-ownership' (*copropriété*). Not only does one have the freehold of the flat but also a share of the freehold of the land upon which it rests. The size of the share is determined by the floor area of the apartment and a number of 10,000th shares are allocated accordingly. The proportion also serves to fix the share of the general service charges payable by each owner.

A big advantage of this co-ownership system is that the owners run the whole show themselves. Whereas in Britain the freeholder can impose the managing agent on the leaseholders, in France the co-owners can hire or fire the *gérant* or *syndic* and remain in charge.

It is important, when buying in a co-ownership, to ask in advance for a copy of the *règlement de copropriété*. This is a weighty document that sets out the technical history of the development (very boring, since it is a recital of the planning permissions in great detail). It also describes each unit with the number of shares each owner acquires. In this way, one knows exactly the voting strength of each owner at the owners' general assembly at which all the major decisions about the running of the development are made. But perhaps most important of all, the covenants that have to be observed by the occupants are listed, very much in the same way as a lease in the UK.

The rules are not imposed by a freeholder, as they would be in this country, since it is the apartment owners themselves who are the freeholders. The covenants usually follow a statutory pattern that makes a lot of sense, and are designed to be in everyone's best interests. For example, no noisy pets are allowed. Washing cannot be hung out of the windows. Window boxes have to be securely fixed and must rest on waterproof containers. And naturally, no noisy parties or playing of loud music at night is allowed.

Although one is not usually permitted to run a business from a residential *copropriété*, a professional person can always use his or her apartment for consultations and put a brass plate outside. Some buyers may not like the idea of being next door to a medical practitioner with a steady stream of visitors.

One important reason for asking to check the *règlement de copropriété* is to ascertain whether or not such a document exists. It is possible, for example, to buy an apartment in an old property which may have been converted into four flats. With so few units, it may have been deemed unnecessary or too expensive to have a notary draw up the document. The danger then is that the rules of how the whole building is to be run is by mutual verbal agreement. This is usually no problem if everyone gets along, but what happens if three of the four flats are bought up by one person? As a majority owner, he or she would rule the roost and you as the fourth owner would have to go along with every decision.

Off-plan

Many purchasers of apartments in France buy before the property is even built. Buying off-plan in this way is necessary if the site is a good one. On the Côte d'Azur, for example, the market is such that all good properties are snapped up before the foundations are even laid. Fortunately, consumer protection legislation in France is such that there is virtually no risk in this exercise.

When a purchaser buying off-plan decides to go ahead, he or she will sign a reservation contract and pay a deposit (usually 5 per cent). He or she will also sign a floor plan and a technical specification. These documents will be countersigned by the developer who will be committed to delivering the property as specified. The purchaser will make payments as and when the building progresses. The usual time delay is one year. Thus, a contract signed in the spring of the current year will allow for delivery by 30 June of the following year. Beware of delivery dates at the end of the season, say in September. That way you lose out on the best part of the year's occupation. Similarly, ski flats should be scheduled for delivery by December and not at the end of the winter.

When buying off-plan, you will be asked to make payments as the building progresses. Usually, the instalments are called in on completion of foundations, on completion of the first floor, the roof, the inner walls, and on final delivery.

The law requires that an architect's certificate be produced to prove that the work has been done. Sometimes the developer or his agent omits to supply the certificate. However, you should always insist upon it before you pay.

Having a house or villa built for you is another way of buying off-plan. An architect-designed house is, of course, an ideal solution. It is expensive, however, and there are many developers who sell houses *clés en mains*. In other words, you select a design and the builder makes all the arrangements, including planning applications, so that when he delivers the property he just hands over the key.

Of course, you need to own some building land first. You might already have your eye on a plot or the builder might be able to supply you with one. If you act independently and buy some land in the country, you will need to ascertain if there will be planning permission. Your first move will be to go to the *mairie* to see if there is a *POS* (*plan d'occupation des sols*) for the *commune*. This is a zoning plan that determines what land, if any, may be developed. If the land you have in mind is constructible, or if the *commune* does not have a *POS*, then you must make your purchase of the plot subject to a satisfactory *certificat d'urbanisme* (planning certificate). On your application you should specify the size of house you envisage.

Building permission

Once you have got your outline permission and have completed the purchase, you must then get building permission for the actual design of house you have in mind (*permis de construire*).

If the construction is over 170 square metres in surface area, or if there is to be an extension to an existing house of over 170 square metres, then the application must be submitted by an architect. Similarly, if the applicant is a company, whether limited or not, an architect must be used irrespective of the size of the operation.

Many British purchasers plan merely to modernise an old farmhouse. This may involve opening up new windows and doorways. Such external alterations need building permission and the dimensions of the new openings must comply with certain set rules. Conversions of barns to dwellings require change of use permission if the barns are free-standing. A barn that adjoins a house and shares the same roof is deemed to be part of the house itself. Septic tanks also need permission. Work inside the house, however, can be freely carried out provided it conforms to standard building regulations. The planning application must be made to the local *mairie* from whom the appropriate forms can be collected. A receipt will be given within 15 days.

If the proposed construction complies with all the rules, including local design regulations, then approval will be forthcoming. This is in fact a passive action on the part of the local authority. If no refusal is issued within two months, the permission is deemed to be granted. The building must then be started within two years. (I am convinced that this is the reason why so many building sites receive a heap of sand and then grind to a halt. The sand heap is proof of commencement and the owner can thus keep his or her permission going until ready to start the real construction work.)

A copy of the planning permission is posted at the *mairie* and the number of the permit must be displayed on the site. Third parties have four months in which to lodge a protest.

Many villa developments are set out in such a way that the developer sells the building plots with a selection of villa designs to choose from. These will all have been cleared with the planning authority in advance.

An advantage with some of these estates is that security is provided with electronically operated main gates and so on. If each house does not have its own pool, there is usually a communal swimming pool and tennis courts, and these are excellent venues for socialising (and improving one's French). One British owner I know said that his children learnt more French in one summer in this way than in a year of sixth form.

Any new building in France, whether architect-designed or constructed by a developer, has to be guaranteed. The law requires a ten-year guarantee on the fabric of the property and a two-year guarantee on the internal installations, such as plumbing and wiring. These guarantees have to be underwritten by an insurance company, so that you are protected even if the builder subsequently ceases to trade.

Taking possession

The procedure for taking possession of a new property in France is carefully set out. The high degree of consumer protection that exists brings with it some rules by which all parties have to abide. Do not think that the developer or builder will simply drop the keys into your palm and let you move in. First, there is the ceremony of the *remise des clés* (delivery of the keys), at the end of which you apply your signature to a declaration confirming that all is in order. If after that all is *not* in order, then any claims you may wish to make will have to be in accordance with accepted practice.

If, after taking possession, you observe any obvious faults, these must be brought to the developer's immediate attention. If faults come to light at a later stage, you will have to claim under the builder's guarantee.

Leaseback

There is one form of co-ownership that is different and quite new. It is called leaseback (*nouvelle propriété*), not to be confused with leasehold. This is a form of ownership that was conceived by a company called Pierre & Vacances. They were heavily involved in creating a new ski resort called Avoriaz, in the French Alps near Geneva. By the end of the 1970s sales were still rather slow after the fall-out of the 1975 recession.

The company took the view that since skiers rarely go on winter sports holidays for more than four weeks in a season, and since there was a growing demand from holiday-makers for ski flats to rent, they would combine the two in a neat formula.

The purchaser would buy the freehold of the apartment but would then rent it back to the company for a period of eleven years, retaining for himself six weeks a year of free occupation. (These weeks would be

spread over high, mid and low seasons.)

By way of rent, the company would reduce the purchase price by 30 per cent, undertake the management, and pick up all the bills for the duration. The scheme proved to be a winner and was subsequently extended to other ski resorts and to many coastal resorts too, not only on the Côte d'Azur but also on the west coast and in Normandy. As a bonus, owners would then be able to exchange any spare weeks for holidays in other resorts in the network. In this way, two weeks could be spent in the French Alps at Christmas, two further weeks in June in, say, St Tropez, and the remaining two weeks for some golf on the Atlantic coast or even for shopping in Paris. There is now an international exchange scheme for similar accommodation elsewhere in the world.

There is much demand from purchasers for this form of ownership, since in addition to the advantages already mentioned, there are other important benefits. First, one is buying an asset for only 70 per cent of its cost. That alone cannot be a bad thing, especially as the 30 per cent reduction is tax free. (On resale, the capital gains tax is assessed at the 100 per cent value, not the discounted price. The difference, and the capital appreciation attached to it, goes straight into the vendor's pocket, untaxed.)

Another important advantage is the freedom from maintenance and upkeep. Not only is the owner spared the trouble but also the expense. In this way, he or she arrives at the apartment for a holiday and need not worry about the niggling matters that beset the owner of a country cottage, say. If you own a place in the country, there is the grass to cut (it often grows waist high between visits), dislodged tiles on the roof to be fixed, people turning up with outstretched hands requesting payment. With a leaseback property, you collect the key from the reception desk and move straight in. Since this type of development is built in conjunction with holiday facilities, you can really feel on holiday the minute the car boot is opened. Leaseback sites all have spacious swimming pools, and the latest ones also have tennis courts, golf courses or even private beaches.

Copropriété financière

Another version of leaseback is called *copropriété financière*. With this system one buys a property, usually an apartment, in the same way as a standard leaseback. The difference is that the discount is smaller, about 15 per cent instead of 30 per cent, and one's occupation rights are reduced to just two weeks in low season. The big advantage, however, is that one earns an annual cash return of 4.5 – 5 per cent tax free. This annual rent is indexed to the cost of living and will rise with inflation.

The result is that the yield on the original capital investment will keep on rising in percentage terms throughout the duration of the nine years' lease.

Naturally, in times of high interest rates, one might think it smarter to keep one's cash in the bank. But the advantage of this investment is that one gains from the capital appreciation of the asset, and at the end of the lease regains possession of the apartment at its full grossed up value, having paid only 85 per cent of the cost in the first place. This formula is of particular interest currently to expatriate purchasers who live in low-interest countries and like the idea of owning an appreciating asset that not only provides tax-free income but is also well managed at someone else's expense.

Rente viagère

A form of ownership that you might come across, especially if dealing direct with a French agent or on reading some of the specialist French property magazines, is that of *rente viagère*. This is a kind of life annuity paid to the vendor. It works like this: the owner of a house, who is likely to be elderly, may want to unlock some of the capital represented by the property. He or she will sell it for a percentage of its value, say 50 per cent.

The balance is then paid as an annuity during the vendor's lifetime. He or she will continue to live in the property and the purchaser will not get possession until he or she dies. It is a gamble by the purchaser on the vendor's life expectancy, an arrangement that I personally find rather macabre.

Timeshare

Timeshare ownership became very popular in the 1970s. Instead of owning the whole property you own the right to occupy a specific week or weeks, usually in perpetuity. You can resell the asset, bequeath it or rent it out for cash if you do not use it.

The concept of timeshare was born in France and not, as many people think, in America. Since, at the time of its birth, many people could not afford to own a holiday home outright, and banks were reluctant to lend for this purpose, the timeshare formula was devised to allow the public access to ownership at a fraction of the cost.

The principle is a good one, but what has now happened is that people are more affluent and banks are falling over themselves to lend money on property. Alternative forms of ownership, such as leaseback, have made inroads into timeshare.

The concept rests or falls on the quality of management. Since a holiday apartment may be owned by as many as 52 different owners (although usually 10–15 owners, some owning multiple weeks) there has to be considerable organisation to ensure that everything runs smoothly. That costs money, and as a result each owner has to pay quite a high management fee for each week he or she owns. Since all the partners are almost without exception absentee owners, there will always be some who do not pay their share. The shortfall then has to be met by the others. In those circumstances, a badly managed block becomes a disaster.

A strong selling point of timeshare is the facility that is offered for exchanging with other timeshares elsewhere in the world. All good timeshare developments subscribe to one of the two main exchange networks. In this way one is not locked into occupying one's own apartment year after year. Again, however, this benefit also brings with it expenses. There will always be a substantial management fee to pay for the privilege of occupying the exchange property. In some countries these fees can be very high.

Holiday property bond

A different, and in my view better, version of timeshare is the holiday property bond. With this system investors do not buy the rights to occupy a particular property for a particular week, but instead they invest in a bond which then allows them to stay in any of the properties which are owned by the scheme. The more you invest, the more occupation rights you have. A clever points system determines what the different weeks in each property are worth.

In this way, an investment of, say, £5000 gives the right to stay in a wide range of locations in different countries. The best-known property bond already owns a *château* in Brittany, cleverly converted into apartments, and has other acquisitions in France coming on stream. By investing £10,000, one would either stay in a larger property or for a longer time in a smaller one. The choice also extends to properties in other countries besides France.

The clever part of the scheme is that not all the funds are invested in property. A sizeable proportion is used to acquire income-producing equity which pays for the management of each property. In this way, the holiday property bond overcomes the main disadvantage of timeshare. No management fee is payable each time one stays in one of the units.

Mobile homes

For a long time, mobile homes have been purchased by British people wishing to have a foothold in France. A number of estates have flourished in the south of France, notably near St Raphaël. As with timeshare, the main advantage of mobile home ownership, which was that of low cost, has been matched by alternative forms of ownership such as leaseback. Land values have risen considerably in the south of France and this makes the arithmetic of caravan park marketing less competitive.

There are two other problems with this form of ownership. A resale is difficult to achieve if you need to get out of the investment with your money back, let alone with some capital appreciation. The second problem is insurance.

Auctions

Some people might consider that buying at auction should be a cheap and clever way to buy a French property. Certainly, houses do get sold in this way, either by banks who have foreclosed on their security or by *notaires* who have to liquidate an estate.

As with all auction sales, one is inevitably in competition with professionals (it is the same in the antique trade). Anyone with local knowledge is going to know more about the circumstances of the sale and it is difficult for an outsider to position himself to be in the right place at the right time in order to pick up a bargain.

Long-term rental

Some people wonder if a long-term rental is not a good halfway house, perhaps before taking the final plunge with a purchase. It is, of course, quite feasible although not always so easy to achieve in practice. This is despite the fact that the French have a much more active private rental sector than we do in Britain.

The reality is that most accommodation available for long-term rent is situated in towns. The tenants naturally occupy these lodgings for their permanent residence. Most British purchasers, however, would want to stay in the country or at least in a small market town. Here the properties that are let tend to be to farm workers and are of low standard in terms of modern conveniences. Small town apartments are usually let to lower paid local employees and again suffer from shortcomings in comfort. It is also true that property owners in the country are wary of outsiders and prefer to let to people they know or who have local connections. It is rare for estate agents outside the cities to handle long-term rents.

Société Civile Immobilière (SCI)

One form of ownership that has recently gained credence is the forming of a company in France. Usually it would be a *Société Civile Immobilière* (*SCI*) or a property-holding company. Many of the 'pundits' who have put forward this idea are a little confused as to the advantages to be gained and they often misread the motives of the potential buyer. The matter is considered further in Chapter 7, page 102.

Chapter 6
Money Matters

BRIGITTE VANDENABEELE and JOHN WARLOW
Brigitte Vandenabeele is the UK representative of Banque Transatlantique. John Warlow is manager of the 'Key to France' service, offered in London by Banque Nationale de Paris.

Opening a French bank account

From time to time, there are people who, having acquired a second home in France, simply cannot be bothered to open a French bank account - too much trouble, they can't understand the language etc - and somehow they manage to exist on a cash/travellers cheque basis.

This is not a particularly wise policy. When the time comes to dispose of their property or to identify its precise value (for tax purposes, succession duties etc), there will be no obvious acceptable records of money movement into France. When exchange control regulations were in force, in order to remove one's sale proceeds from France, one had to prove that the funds to buy, construct, repair etc actually emanated from a non-resident, non-French, external source before they could be cleared for external payment. Although such regulations have been relaxed, it is worth maintaining banking proof of the investment.

Since January 1990, there have been no restrictions on the movement of funds between Britain and France, when they are handled by the intermediary of banks and recognised financial organisations.

Our advice always is that you do need a French franc bank account: thus you will easily be able to direct your sterling funds into the French banking system; you will be able to pay suppliers via cheques; have your electricity, gas or telephone accounts settled via direct debits; pay your property taxes by cheque; obtain cash over the counter of your bank's branches nationwide; and, via your bank's charge card (*Carte Bleue Visa* etc) pay for restaurant, hotel and garage expenditure. The amounts will be directly debited at the month end. You will have to have a French bank account if you take out a loan in France - the lending bank will want to debit that account with your regular repayments of capital and interest.

The type of account you open depends on whether or not you are a resident of France. According to an article of 29 December 1989 in the *Journal Officiel*, a person is considered resident if he has his main centre of interest in France. This is a rather vague definition, translated word for word, but it means that France has to be the place where you live (even in an hotel or rented accommodation) or work.

So the person who goes to work or retires in France becomes resident more or less from the time of arrival. It is necessary, however, to produce evidence that you have a job or a copy of the application for a *carte de séjour* to be able to open a resident's account.

In all other cases (for example, if you are buying a second home only) a non-resident account will be sufficient.

Where to open a bank account

- Locally.
- From London. Most French banks operating in London should be able to provide that facility. The account may be managed and held from the head office in France but one would have access to a network of branches or affiliated banks in France.

How:

- An account can be opened by correspondence. Banks will usually provide translations. However, the signature will have to be witnessed by a solicitor.
- In person at the branch or representative office of the French bank. A valid passport will have to be presented.

Operating a bank account

(a) *No cheque guarantee card will be issued*, as the procedure is unknown in France. It has to be borne in mind that it is a serious offence to incur an overdraft where there is no prior agreement with the bank. The bank may decide in that case to withdraw the use of a cheque book. One is listed as an *interdit bancaire* and registered as such with the Banque de France, preventing the opening of another bank account and access to a cheque book for the next 12 months.

It should also be noted that cheques can only be stopped if they have been lost or stolen.

(b) *Obtaining* a *Carte Bleue (national) or Carte Bleue Visa (international)*
This is a charge card, not a credit card with deferred payment. A statement is sent to the card holder each month and the amount debited directly from the bank account by the bank.

It can be used as a service till card in more than 11,500 service tills in *any* bank, as it is accepted by all major banks. No interest is paid for that service.

(c) *How to credit an account in France*
The quickest method is to arrange a transfer from bank to bank. However, this method can be costly. It is also possible to ask the British bank or building society to issue a bankers' draft.

The simplest way, however, is to send a cheque in sterling. Ten to 12 days minimum should be allowed for the cheque to be cleared before drawing against it.

Eurocheques or French franc travellers cheques are another easy and quick method. However, a commission may be payable for Eurocheques.

Generally speaking, the clearance of cheques can take longer than in the UK. Sufficient time should be allowed before drawing funds.

(d) *Standing orders/direct debits*
It is customary to arrange for the payment of electricity, gas, telephone, water bills etc, by direct debits. Forms are available from banks. A *relève d'identité bancaire*, provided by the bank and giving all details concerning the account to be debited, is sent to the relevant board.

A last word about the French banking system. Services such as:

- monthly statements
- cheque books
- direct debits

are free of charge. However, cheque books and credit cards must be sent by registered mail and the cost is borne by the client.

Bank statements will show the *date de valeur*. This is when debits and credits take effect, and is the date to take into consideration when assessing the true position of an account.

Financing the purchase of a property in France

Once a decision has been made to buy in France, suitable answers will have to be found on how to finance such an acquisition. Should one pay cash or borrow? Furthermore, and the object of endless debates, should one borrow in pounds or in French francs, in the UK or in France?

There is a range of financial options available and, as might be expected, a range of financial institutions, both French and British, eager to offer their solution to those needs.

When these options are studied, it will be found – in general – that two

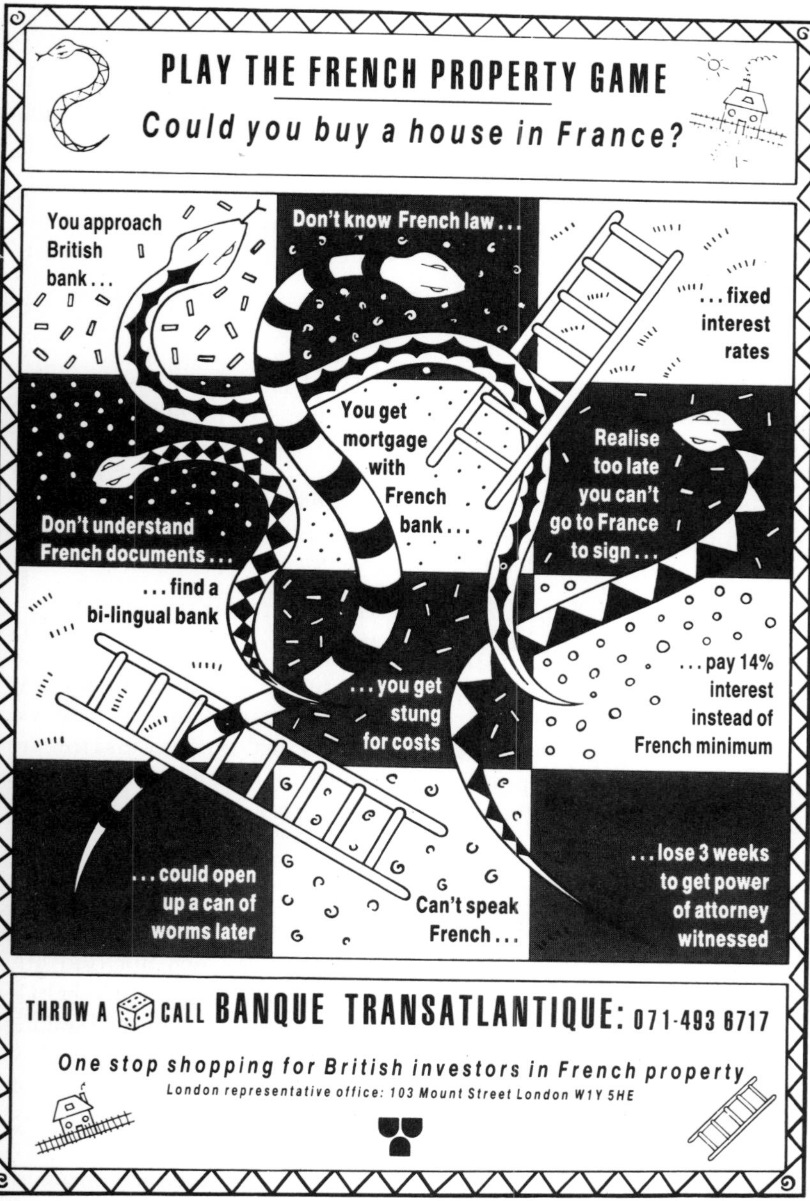

PLAY THE FRENCH PROPERTY GAME
Could you buy a house in France?
You approach British bank...
Don't know French law...
...fixed interest rates
You get mortgage with French bank...
Realise too late you can't go to France to sign...
Don't understand French documents...
...find a bi-lingual bank
...you get stung for costs
...pay 14% interest instead of French minimum
...could open up a can of worms later
Can't speak French...
...lose 3 weeks to get power of attorney witnessed
THROW A CALL BANQUE TRANSATLANTIQUE: 071-493 6717
One stop shopping for British investors in French property
London representative office: 103 Mount Street London W1Y 5HE

alternatives are offered; a UK alternative and a French alternative, that is to say:

- a borrowing in sterling, in the UK, against the security of a UK asset (the family home, for example) and at UK rates of interest;
- a borrowing in francs, in France, against the security of the French property being purchased, and at French domestic rates of interest.

There are variations on these which will be considered in due course, but for the moment let us concentrate on the two classic methods which are generally available.

UK loan

This is basically quite simple: a standard UK mortgage from a UK-based institution (ie building society, bank or specialist mortgage company - British or French), which may remortgage the UK home or offer an equity release scheme to allow you to finance your needs in France. You simply buy francs with the sterling loan and arrange for the French bank to receive the funds with the appropriate instructions to pay the *notaire.* Do transfer more than the *notaire* requests because:

(a) the French bank may take a commission off your transfer; and
(b) funds will be needed for future expenses.

The interest rate will be that available in the UK market and the repayment may be on a standard repayment of capital/interest basis, via an endowment policy or via a pension plan. Legal expenses and fees are in accordance with UK practice. Remember, however, that there is no UK tax relief on the interest paid on this borrowing.

French loan

Obviously, to the British buyer, the French alternative will be less familiar and potentially more difficult. First, you will not find any building society or the French equivalent able to give any help - mortgage finance in France is primarily provided through the banking system. Second, it will certainly be more difficult if you cannot speak or read French and are dealing with a local French bank in the region where you are buying with whom long-distance correspondence may be somewhat tedious.

Therefore, a number of French banks have established specialist teams in Britain who can act as an interface to the French domestic banking system. The staff are bilingual, explanations can be given in English and documentation provided in both languages - obviously, though, the various procedures have to respect French law and all legal documents must be in French.

Major differences between French and British types of mortgage

(a) Mortgages in French francs are offered at a *fixed* rate of interest over the term selected.

Variable and progressive rates can be offered at the request of clients but this is the exception rather than the rule for buyers in France, and is viewed as an expensive way of borrowing. It is generally advisable only for young buyers at the beginning of their career with restricted financial means in the early years.

But what happens if a client takes a mortgage when the rate is high, as in 1981–82 when it was around 17 per cent? The answer is that, due to competition, banks may be compelled to renegotiate such rates. However, the contrary is not true: an offer signed at a rate of 10 per cent will remain fixed, even if the rate goes up.

(b) The term of the mortgage is shorter: up to 15 or, perhaps, 20 years.

(c) The mortgages available are normally of the straightforward repayment method. Therefore, with the fixed interest rate offered, you will know exactly what your monthly repayment amounts to. This will include capital, interest and life, health and invalidity insurance (where applicable) and will be constant over the period selected. A schedule of repayment will be provided so that at any time over the term, you will know the capital outstanding to be reimbursed. As a corollary, pension and endowment mortgages are not as commonly available as they are in the UK, although the indications are that this situation is changing.

(d) The bank will not ask for a survey, although you can choose to have an inspection carried out independently. The loan is based on 70–80 per cent of the purchase price (without expenses and legal fees), as stipulated in the *compromis de vente*. So, if the expenses and legal fees come to an additional 20 per cent, for example, and you take out a loan to cover 80 per cent of the price of the house, you will have to find the equivalent of 40 per cent yourself.

(e) The amount of the loan granted will not be calculated by using multiples of income. Instead, it will be considered that the monthly repayment of loans contracted in France (and in the UK if applicable) should not exceed 30 per cent of your gross monthly income.

It is necessary to identify the borrower's revenues, from whatever source, before tax (ie after deduction of payments for social security,

State or employer pension). Then the total of the borrower's present commitments to service his term liabilities (eg a mortgage and the life insurance related to that mortgage, car loan, house improvement loan, rent if he does not own the home, and any payments under a court order subsequent to a divorce) are added to the costs of servicing the new French mortgage loan. If that new total is less than 30 per cent of his net pre-tax revenues the borrower is, *prima facie*, within the bank's lending criteria.

If there is to be more than one borrower or the spouse is also earning, it is still possible to lend – the calculation being based on combined cash flow. However, a bank would not want to lend to more than three joint borrowers.

(f) French banks in France will normally require the services of a *notaire* acting on their behalf. This *notaire* will ensure that all necessary documents relating to the loan are forwarded to his or her colleague for inclusion in the conveyance and that the conveyance is in order before the funds are released by the bank, thus providing the client with an added protection but at no extra cost (as *notaires* share their fee).

The costs to be incurred by a client taking a loan in France are twofold:

1. An arrangement fee payable to the bank usually of 1 per cent of the mortgage with a maximum of FF 2500 plus VAT at 18.60 per cent.
2. The cost of registering the charge against the property at the *Bureau de Conservation des Hypothèques* (Land Registry). This registration is done by the *notaire* and the cost is therefore payable to him and will appear on the final invoice as '*frais d'enregistrement, frais de prêt*' etc. A sliding scale of such fees is available.

Types of mortgage available in France

These vary according to the nature of the purchase.

(a) The most common and straightforward is a repayment mortgage granted for the *purchase of an existing property*.

At this point it must be emphasised that any potential purchaser ought to be aware of his rights under French consumer protection legislation. In July 1979, the Loi Scrivener was enacted: it provides the basis on which a lender and a borrower do business and the rules under which private residential property is purchased where the buyer is buying with the aid of a bank loan (see page 84).

The buyer/borrower will have been asked, when signing the *compromis de vente* (the agreement to purchase) or reservation contract, whether he will need to obtain bank finance. If so, the agreement will include this as a precondition of the purchase and will probably identify a one-month time-limit (minimum) within which the buyer must obtain the loan. If a loan is refused, he can withdraw from the contract without penalty. If the buyer does not state that a loan is required, he should be asked to certify that fact in the agreement and will not be entitled to the law's protection should he reverse that decision and decide to apply for a loan.

This establishes one time-limit. The other principal time-limit will be the date of signature of the *acte de vente* (the conveyance which, if there is to be a loan, will include the security arrangements and other loan conditions) and this date will be around two months from signature of the purchase agreement.

An additional requirement of the July 1979 law is that a private client borrower is not permitted to accept the terms and conditions of a bank loan without the expiry of a ten-day cooling-off period. The bank must send him a letter of offer of which the borrower acknowledges receipt. On the eleventh day thereafter the borrower may accept it (he has 30 days in which to do this) and return it to the lender, who will hold the loan available for four months (it can be used over a longer period if it relates to a building project).

Not until the accepted loan offer is returned to the bank can the bank instruct the *notaire* to draw up the relevant security documentation. Thus, it could be a further one or two weeks before the *notaire* is able to arrange signature of the conveyance and request release of the loan by the bank. Remember, the *notaire* will also require the buyer to send the balance of the purchase price, as well as his fees and other expenses by the date agreed.

It can be understood, therefore, that, if a time-scale of eight weeks from signing the purchase agreement to signature of the conveyance is agreed, there is ample scope for delays to arise and the time-limit to be broken. For example, as a borrower not known to the French bank, the buyer will have to provide an up-to-date explanation of his financial situation - revenues, annual commitments on term lending or other liabilities (as noted earlier), assets and liabilities. The bank obviously has to take up references from employer, bank and perhaps accountant - and often employers are slow to respond and accountants do not have up-to-date financial information available.

Equally, if the borrower has not made the application for a loan until, say, ten days after signature of the purchase agreement, it will be almost impossible for the lender to have adequately checked him out, sent an offer letter, allowed a cooling-off period, instructed the *notaire* regarding the loan's terms and conditions with sufficient time to allow completion within an eight-week time-scale.

Therefore, it is strongly recommended that when a purchase is negotiated and if mortgage finance is required, one aims for completion

at least 10–12 weeks from signature of the agreement to buy. Also, at that stage do not book up any holidays, ferry or hotel; do not organise the removal van in the anticipation that the keys to the new property will be handed over on the date proposed some two and a half months in the future.

(b) Loans available for the *purchase of a property off-plan or being built.*

Again, such loans would be offered at a fixed rate of interest even though the funds would be released by stages as payments become due according to the stages described in the conveyance and against the presentation of an architect's certificate. This period is known as the *période d'anticipation* during which interest only is payable on a monthly basis on the amount which has been released by the bank. The length of such a period will depend therefore on the time needed by the builder to complete his work as stipulated in the *contrat de réservation.*

Once the final payment has been made, the mortgage will reach its *période d'amortissement* where the client will repay, normally, capital, interest and insurance, hence a fixed amount over the term chosen for the loan.

If the bank were to intervene at completion (when usually a 30 per cent payment is required) such a loan would be registered in the conveyance document. Should the bank only intervene in the later stages, an *acte de prêt* would be prepared by the *notaire.*

(c) *Purchase of land only.*

Such loans are available on a shorter term (five years maximum). However, should a further loan be required later on for the building of a property on the land, on a longer term, it is possible to ensure that the former loan (for land purchase) be integrated to the later on the longer-term basis.

(d) *Loans for repair work/improvements etc.*

Full estimates of the work to be carried out are required. The bank will lend 70–80 per cent of the total amount required and payments will be made directly to the builders upon presentation of an invoice. Rates can be slightly higher.

(e) *Bridging loans* are often required by British people selling their UK homes and experiencing delays in finalising the sale.

A charge will be registered on the French property for the duration of the loan. However, should the exchange of contract stage have been reached in the UK, it may prove unnecessary to register a charge in France. Such loans are granted over a period from a few months to one or two years maximum. Interest only is payable (with insurance). The capital is repaid on completion of the sale in the UK.

(f) *Property developer loans.*

In view of the slackening of the British market, some British property developers have shown an interest in the French market and registered as *marchands de biens* (property agents). Special loans are available for such short-term purchases where a quick turnover of properties is sought. Two possibilities exist.

1. Either an overdraft facility granted by the French bank over a period of one year, renewable, with interest only repayment at a fixed rate to be negotiated with the bank and on the strength of a letter of guarantee given by a British bank to the French one. Therefore, the charge is secured on the British assets.
2. Or the same facility but with a charge registered on the French property(ies) by the French lender. This will have to be repeated every time a property is sold, unless one property is kept as a security and the funds released are used to buy and sell others.

Editor's note.

(g) A third option is the 'Anglo-French' loan.

One or two French and British financial institutions are now offering British-style mortgages (including endowment and pension-linked, as well as repayment, loans), using the French property as security. The loans are arranged in the UK under English law and are administered in the UK. Some loans can be transacted in either French francs or sterling, with the facility to switch currencies. Payments can be made in sterling, direct from a British bank account, and some lenders offer free currency conversion.

Borrowing is based on income multiples which, as we have seen, is rarely, if ever, a feature of the French option. Some of the schemes offer a loan term of up to 25 years. Check individual schemes for both the minimum and the maximum you are allowed to borrow. If you intend to become resident in France, you should take professional advice on your position with regard to income tax relief.

Available currencies

The currencies available for mortgages raised with a French bank are outlined below.

Mortgages in French francs

As we have seen, their interest rates are fixed for residential properties and are particularly attractive to British clients at the moment, when the remortgage of a property in the UK would prove an expensive exercise.

There are other considerations, too. The property purchased is in France, will be paid for in francs and the purchase will be governed by French law. It therefore makes sense to consider the use of an FF mortgage secured on that same property. Such properties are often rented for the holidays, thus generating French francs which can be partly used to repay the loan.

Lastly, should the property be sold, the interest paid will be taken into account for the calculation of capital gains tax (for secondary residence).

The main element of risk rests with the effect of exchange rate fluctuations between the pound and French franc on monthly repayments.

However, transfer of the funds could be made on a half-yearly or yearly basis, to take advantage of favourable rates. Some French banks will offer interest-bearing current accounts for non-residents.

Such fluctuations are limited in scale. If one looks back over the last ten years, variations never exceeded 10 per cent, taking FF 10 to the pound as a reference figure.

Lastly, sooner rather than later, Britain will join the European Monetary System (EMS) which will restrict such risks even further. After all, sterling already accounts for 19 per cent of the basket of currencies in the calculation of the European Currency Unit (ECU).

Mortgages in other currencies, Swiss francs, US dollars or ECUs

These facilities may be attractive to people with access to such currencies (for example, a British citizen working in the United States and paid in dollars) or those with the knowledge and will to take advantage of the currency market.

Such loans are at a variable rate of interest, based on PIBOR (Paris International Banking Rates of Exchange) plus 2 per cent, reviewed every six months with repayments on a half-yearly basis. Interest is payable on the decreasing balance of outstanding capital. Capital repayment can be either constant or progressive according to the needs of the client. It is possible to revert to a French franc mortgage or eventually shift to another currency. Check whether your French bank offers this facility.

Arranging a French mortgage

Arranging for a mortgage in France should be an easy procedure, given the proper advice and a safe one in view of the strict consumer protection laws. We can only recommend that proper advice is sought.

Some banks, on occasion, are able to be more flexible than others and produce a totally 'impossible' answer to a problem: the converse is also true. As your needs are discussed with different lenders, you will also be met with a range of differing styles of quotation. Some will identify the 'bottom line' costs of borrowing (total monthly payments, fees etc chargeable) while others will simply tell the borrower his interest rate (perhaps with, perhaps without, insurance premium).

What has to be done is to try to compare like with like and also assess the variety of levels of service they can all provide - some lenders, for example, will not help with the opening of bank accounts, property insurance, legal and tax advice.

Chapter 7

Duties, Taxes and Inheritance Law

ROBERT URQUHART
Robert Urquhart is a partner in De Pinna, Scorers & John Venn, a long-established firm of notaries of the City of London. He is responsible for the firm's French Department, which advises private and corporate clients on all aspects of property purchase in France, and is a leading authority on French law.

If you own or are contemplating the purchase of a property in France, you will certainly at some time or another be liable to pay one or more French duties and taxes. This chapter identifies and describes the main taxes payable by a British purchaser of residential property in France. There is also a section on the French law of inheritance.

General information

1. Some taxes in France are collected and paid automatically on the occurrence of certain events. For example, on a purchase, transfer duty is payable as part of the purchase costs to the *notaire* who, in turn, accounts for it to the French Tax Administration.

   The general tax system in France is, however, on a declaratory basis, not all that dissimilar to the US system. A British purchaser of property in France with income arising should not therefore wait to be assessed. It is up to the taxpayer to return details of income arising to the French Revenue. It is not an excuse to say 'I didn't know'.

2. Even though it may be tempting to compare the legal and tax systems in France with those of some southern European countries, this would be a serious mistake. France is an ultra-modern twentieth-century state with laws and tax laws to match. Some of the anti-avoidance provisions contained in recent French legislation go beyond anything we have in the UK. The French know about tax. It is they who invented the concept of value added tax!

3. Although the French tax system may at first glance seem somewhat lax, do not be deceived by appearances: if a taxpayer is caught defrauding the French Revenue, he will be pursued relentlessly.

Remember that your property is in France and can, and will, be seized to satisfy a debt to the Revenue.

4. The taxes and duties facing a British purchaser of property to be used as a second home in France are numerous, complicated and their applicability is unpredictable.

Duties and taxes on purchase

On a purchase of residential property in France, costs, as a rule of thumb, are either roughly 10 per cent or roughly 3 per cent.

10 per cent

On any purchase of residential property in France, transfer duty (*droit de mutation*) of approximately 7.5 per cent is levied on the purchase price and is payable by the purchaser. As this duty is made up of communal, regional and departmental taxes, the total amount varies slightly from area to area. The difference between 7.5 and 10 per cent costs is made up of stamp duty, Land Registry charges, fees of the notary, and VAT on the notary's fees.

3 per cent

However, where one is purchasing a new property off-plan or within five years from structural completion, the sale is generally within the *TVA* (or VAT) net and there is only a transfer duty of 0.6 per cent payable by the purchaser. If stamp duty, Land Registry charges and fees of the notary are added, the total is approximately 3 per cent. There is no transfer duty as above because *TVA*, at 18.6 per cent, is deemed to be already included in the price.

On purchases of agricultural land, the rate of transfer duty is 14.6 per cent, on the purchase of commercial buildings, the rate is 16.6 per cent, in addition, building land can carry a *TVA* rate of 13 per cent.

Purchasers are sometimes asked to make 'black' or 'under the table' payments by under-declaring the purchase price and paying the balance in cash to the vendor. Needless to say, this is illegal and the risk of being found out is very great. It will also store up problems for the purchaser at a later date when the property is sold. Do not get involved in transactions of this kind.

Rates

There are basically two of these: *taxe d'habitation* if the property is not let or *taxe professionelle* if it is, and *tax foncière*. They are both payable annually to the local authority, the *taxe d'habitation* being payable by the occupant of the property as at the previous 1 January.

Where you are purchasing a property off-plan, assuming the appropriate application is made, a tax holiday from paying the *taxe foncière* is granted for two years. By comparison with the UK, the amount of both these taxes taken together is somewhat less than our community charge.

Income taxes

Individuals, who are resident in France for tax purposes, are liable for French income tax on the entirety of their worldwide income.

French income tax rates

The top rate of French income tax is currently 56 per cent. The level at which this rate applies depends on the personal circumstances of the taxpayer.

French income tax on second homes

This concerns owners of properties in France who are not fiscally domiciled there.

Individuals

The general rule is given in article 164c of the French general tax code.

> *Article 164c CGI (translation)*
> 'Persons who do not have their fiscal domicile in France, but who have one or more residences there, in whatever manner and whether held directly or held through a third party, shall be subject to income tax assessed on a base equal to three times the real rental value of such property unless their income from French sources shall be greater than such base, in which case that income will serve as the base.'

The general rule, therefore, is that all non-residents owning residential property in France are subject to income tax on three times the deemed rental value. This is not a recent provision and has been in force since 1976. However, a person resident in the UK can avoid this tax under the Anglo-French double tax treaty, which prevents such a deemed tax being levied. On the other hand, a resident of the Bahamas, Jersey or Hong Kong would not be protected and would risk a deemed assessment under article 164c.

Although a UK individual resident owner of property in France may avoid a deemed assessment, any income actually derived from the property, and it must be emphasised any income, wheresoever it is paid, is deemed to be income arising in France. It must be declared to the

French Revenue within two months from the end of the French financial year which corresponds to the calendar year. The tax computation is fairly complicated, but a non-resident would generally be taxed at the rate of 25 per cent on the net income from the property after deduction of allowable expenses and expenditure.

The income declared and arising in France must also be declared on your usual tax return to the UK Revenue. Under the double tax treaty with France, a credit will be given against the UK assessment of tax for any income tax paid in France.

Letting furnished residential accommodation in France is itself a commercial activity and French *TVA* (VAT) must be charged on the rent at the rate of 5.5 per cent. This is not recoverable under the double tax treaty.

Corporation tax and companies

Companies incorporated in a tax haven, or in a place that does not have a full double tax treaty with France, will pay an annual tax equal to 3 per cent of the market value of the property owned by the offshore company. This provision, in one form or another, has been around for nearly 20 years. It means that if you wish to hide your identity behind, say, a Jersey company, you may do so, but it will cost 3 per cent of the capital value each year, without deduction, for the privilege.

There is an exemption from paying the 3 per cent tax if the owning company has its registered office and is managed in a country that has a full double tax treaty with France.

Britain is such a country. Although a UK company can avoid paying the 3 per cent tax, this does not by any means absolve it from paying tax in France.

A UK company will need to file before 15 May in each year a special form showing the value of the property as at the previous 1 January, the names and addresses of all shareholders, and other relevant information. In addition, a UK company is liable to the minimum corporation tax charge in France, which is currently FF5000, and shareholders and/or directors may be liable to a benefit-in-kind assessment. It will also probably be necessary to use French accountants and a fiscal agent, who must be appointed to deal with the Revenue on behalf of the foreign company. All in all, costs and taxes in France, payable by a UK company owning residential property there, are likely to be greater than one would think.

Close companies

From the UK side, it is likely that a UK company formed for the purpose of acquiring a residential property in France will be a 'close' company within the meaning of section 414 of the Income and Corporation Taxes Act 1988. This is broadly defined as being a UK resident company which is under the control of five or fewer participators.

There is specific legislation which deals with close companies and which seeks to ensure that participators of close companies do not receive benefits which are untaxed. The Inland Revenue in the UK will therefore seek to treat any benefit as a distribution from the company where participators are provided with living or other accommodation.

In short, where a distribution is treated as having been made to a participator, the company is liable to account for advance corporation tax on the distribution and the participator is assessed to a higher rate of tax, if he is a higher rate taxpayer. The Inland Revenue can go further than this and classify certain persons as 'deemed directors' to bring them within the tax rules, for example where there are shadow directors acting on the instructions of the person/persons using the property.

The value of the benefit-in-kind of the accommodation in any period is the rent which would have been payable if the premises had been let at an annual and market rental.

Thus, it can safely be assumed that the Inland Revenue will, by one or more sections of the Taxes Act, be able to levy a substantial income tax liability on a UK resident individual who is provided with the use of a French property through a UK resident company of which he is either a director, a deemed director or a shareholder.

It will be seen therefore that the use of non-French companies to hold residential property in France can have serious tax consequences in France and the UK. Such use is usually wholly inappropriate to the average British person buying a holiday home in France.

In creating any corporate or tax structures where France is concerned, it is a good idea to bear in mind that as a general rule, a French solution to a French property or tax problem is generally more effective than an English solution grafted on to the French problem.

Wealth tax

Wealth tax (*impôt de solidarité sur la fortune* or *ISF*) was reintroduced on 1 January 1989, having been abolished some two years previously when it was called *impôt sur les grandes fortunes*. This tax affects all persons whose assets in France exceed FF4.13 million in 1990 but the tax relates only to individuals, not companies. It is up to a taxpayer to declare the value of his or her assets in France each year only if those assets exceed FF4.13 million. The tax for the first tranche above FF4.13 million is one half of 1 per cent, payable each year.

Tax on the sale of property

On the sale of a property in France, there is French capital gains tax. This is payable by non-residents on the basis of 33⅓ per cent of the net gain after a coefficient to allow for inflation has been applied to the original purchase price. If the property has been held longer than two years, a further tapering is allowed so that, as a general rule, allowances against capital gains tax in France are fairly generous. Clearly, an English resident must also make a return in England for capital gains tax purposes, and any gains tax paid in France is of course allowable against the English CGT assessment under the double tax treaty.

An exemption from French capital gains tax is currently available to EC residents (but not residents of France) selling their first secondary residence in France available for use by them since purchase and held for more than five years. There is also an exemption if it is the first sale of a secondary residence in France, whether held for more or less than five years, where resale is caused by compelling family reasons.

Where an English company is concerned, the 33⅓ per cent calculation is used in the first instance, and thereafter a 42 per cent charge to corporation tax is made on the residual difference between the sale price and the written down purchase price over the period the property has been held. In addition, there may also be withholding tax at 15 per cent if there has been a distribution of the proceeds to the shareholders.

All non-residents of France selling property must, in addition to paying capital gains tax, appoint a guarantor to the French Revenue who is responsible for any capital gains tax that the vendor might be deemed to owe the Revenue. This guarantor can only be (a) the purchaser (if resident in France and if willing), (b) a person resident in France who is willing, or (c) a bank operating in France. It is possible in many cases to obtain an exemption from appointing a guarantor, but the exemption must be applied for.

Succession duty or inheritance tax

In France, succession duty is payable by beneficiaries; indeed, by each beneficiary rather than by the estate. The rate of tax varies, depending on the blood or marital relationship between the beneficiary and the deceased. Taking children and spouses first, each child or spouse has a threshold of FF275,000 and thereafter there is a sliding scale up to 40 per cent maximum. The scale does not, however, rise above 20 per cent unless the net estate exceeds FF3.4 million or £340,000 approximately. As between brothers and sisters, the threshold is only FF10,000 and the rate is 35 per cent up to FF150,000 and 45 per cent above that, a considerable difference. Between collaterals to the fourth degree, the rate is flat at 55 per cent, and between persons who are not related by blood, the rate is a flat 60 per cent.

Inter vivos gifts are taxed in the same way.

As a general rule, therefore, leave property in France to your spouse and children and take advantage of the relatively low inheritance tax rates.

The French law of inheritance

The French law of inheritance is one of the areas that causes most problems when second homes are purchased across the Channel. To understand it, you need to have a basic grasp of the difference between an estate where there is a will, known as a testate estate, and where there is no will, known as an intestate estate.

In England, where there is no will, the law itself makes certain dispositions of property and in the case of a surviving husband or wife with children, English law will see to it that a very large part of the estate will go to the surviving spouse. In France, it is very different. Where there is no will, all that goes to the surviving spouse is one quarter in life interest. By English standards, this is derisory. Anyone considering emigrating to France must make sure that their spouse is protected by will.

Where wills are concerned, English law does not restrict in any way a person's freedom to leave assets to anyone they choose. French law does. Certain classes of beneficiaries have what is known as a legal reserve. Assets are divided into two categories: immovables or movables. An immovable is land or a house. Movables are everything else: shares in companies, money in the bank, cars and so on. As between England and France, movables will pass in accordance with the law of the country where a person dies domiciled. Immovables will pass in accordance with the law where the property is situated.

Take the case of an English couple resident and domiciled in England owning a second home in France. The husband dies domiciled in England. His entire estate is governed by and is wound up in accordance with the law of his domicile, ie English law, *except* his property in France which is dealt with in accordance with French law.

It is because French law applies to French land that problems connected with the legal reserve are encountered. The legal reserve affects children only, or if there are no children, then any living parents of a deceased person. Children include illegitimate or adopted children and the age of the children is of no relevance. No one else has a legal reserve in French law.

The legal reserve for children is as follows: where there is one child, that child's legal reserve is one half of the estate; where there are two children, those children's legal reserve is two-thirds divided equally between them; where there are three or more children, the legal reserve is three-quarters divided equally between the children. French law decrees that not less than those shares must go to children.

If, therefore, an Englishman with two children owns a property in France and leaves the property to his wife, the legal reserve of the children is infringed as their right is two-thirds and the maximum that can be left to the surviving spouse is one-third. The gift to the wife would be reduced accordingly, unless the children renounced theirs. You should bear in mind, however, that if the children renounce their entitlements, more inheritance duty is payable as (in this example) two thresholds each of FF275,000 are 'lost'.

Many problems arise from the application of the French legal reserve, mainly because so few people in the UK know of its existence or its effects. This is changing and there is much more awareness of the legal reserve, which in certain circumstances can cause hardship or involve an estate in the payment of substantial costs and duties.

The main areas to be concerned about are where a person or a couple buy a property in France and then one or both of them dies leaving minor children. A minor is any person under 18 years of age. For various technical reasons, it can prove very difficult to sell a property in France owned by an English minor. It may well be that a property can become literally unsaleable until the youngest minor in a family becomes 18 years old.

The other area which can cause problems is where a couple buy a property and one or both partners have children by previous marriages who may or may not get on with one another. In those circumstances, the effect of the legal reserve means that, after the death of the first of the couple, the survivor ends up owning the property with the children of his or her partner's former marriage.

It is not generally recommended that groups club together to buy properties, be they two or more couples, groups of friends etc. This is a recipe for expensive litigation at one extreme or legal fees and costs as soon as one party wishes to pull out at the other.

How does one minimise the effects of French inheritance law?

There are a number of techiques that can be used, such as the tontine clause or the use of a French company, as outlined below. It should be emphasised that these techniques should not be primarily regarded as a way of defeating the legal reserve of children. If you set out with the deliberate intention of defeating a child's legal reserve, this could be construed as a fraud against the estate and the child's rights.

It is much more acceptable to endeavour to postpone the effect of the legal reserve or to organise your estate so that the effect of the legal reserve is minimised. From the inheritance tax point of view, it is often cheaper to do it this way as well. The most effective solution is often to let your children have ownership or title on your death of the greater part of your French property, but make arrangements so that your spouse will have, and continue to have, control and use of the property for his or her life.

La clause tontine

This clause can only be inserted in the conveyance at the time of purchase, not afterwards. The effect of the tontine clause is that on the death of one of the persons having bought under the tontine clause (usually a husband and wife), it operates retrospectively to vest the entire property in the survivor. The survivor then has complete freedom to dispose of the property as he or she wishes. However:

1. A sale of a property when both parties to the tontine clause are alive is only possible if both consent; if one declines to sell, the other cannot force the sale.
2. In the event of a matrimonial dispute between persons under the tontine clause, a court would have great difficulty in making an order in relation to the property because, so long as both parties to the tontine are living, there is uncertainty as to who is the owner. A court could therefore only order a sale by both parties.
3. The inheritance tax position is as follows:
   (a) On the death of the first party, there is for tax purposes a deemed transfer of half the property, and French inheritance duty will therefore be payable on this half.
   (b) If there is a large difference in age between the parties to the tontine, the French Revenue may seek to classify the tontine as a gift and this could have serious tax consequences, especially if the persons to the tontine are not related by blood or marriage.

There are therefore legal and tax disadvantages as well as advantages to the use of a tontine clause.

A French Société Civile Immobilière (SCI)

French companies are broadly classified as *sociétés de personnes* (mainly *sociétés civiles*) or *sociétés de capitaux*. *Sociétés civiles* can be property-holding companies or professional partnerships. *Sociétés de capitaux* are trading companies. The distinction is made for taxation purposes.

Shares in a *Société Civile Immobilière (SCI)* (property-holding company) are movables and the devolution of such shares is not governed by the mandatory French inheritance rules, provided the shareholders are not domiciled in France.

Two or more persons purchasing a property in France can therefore opt to form an *SCI* to hold a property before or after purchase. If this is done after purchase, transfer duty of 1 per cent of the value of the property transferred to the *SCI*, *droit d'apport*, will be levied, plus notarial and Land Registry fees.

Property owners in France using an *SCI* will own not property but shares, which will pass in accordance with the law of a person's domicile. The advantage is that the shares may be left, for example, to children, but with the surviving spouse retaining a sufficient majority shareholding to make all important decisions. The practical effect is that the children's legal reserve is satisfied, but that all important control is vested in the surviving spouse.

An *SCI* has these further consequences:

- It is best used by one or more individual persons resident in a country that has a full double tax treaty with France.
- It is transparent for tax purposes, that is to say it is not subject to French corporation tax. The shareholders are therefore in roughly the same position (in relation, for example, to capital gains tax or income tax on letting) as they would be if they held title direct.
- If the *SCI* is managed outside France, which in the circumstances of UK residents forming an *SCI* to own property in France is likely, the shareholders will need to make an annual disclosure to claim a tax exemption from the French Revenue.
- Share transfers carry a duty of 4.8 per cent of the value transferred which compares favourably with a transfer cost of approximately 10 per cent for transfer of the land.

Thus a *Société Civile Immobilière* can minimise the effect of the legal reserve rules and in many cases is an effective way of holding property in France.

Wills

An English will is usually just as effective in dealing with your French property as a French will. Neither an English nor a French will can change the underlying legal reserve position. French wills are usually handwritten in your own hand and in French and so are best avoided unless you know what you are doing. Consider an English codicil (to your English will) dealing exclusively with your French property.

Gift between husband and wife (*donation entre époux*)
It is sometimes suggested that English purchasers of a residential property in France should enter into a *donation entre époux* which might in some undefined way overcome the inheritance difficulties outlined above. This is a popular misconception. A gift between spouses will not, and indeed cannot, change the underlying rules relating to the French legal reserve. For practical purposes, a gift between spouses can merely confer on the survivor of them the same benefits and shares that are available using a will. As in French law a gift between spouses can be revoked at any time by the person who made the gift (as indeed a will can be changed at any time during the life of the person who made it), a gift between spouses is not an absolute gift at all and although there used to be tax advantages available for using such a gift, this is no longer so.

These are but some of a large number of techniques that are commonly used to deal with the inheritance and tax aspects of a secondary home in France. Before adopting any technique to minimise or postpone the French legal reserve rules and/or deal with the taxation consequences, it cannot be emphasised too strongly or too often that property professional advice must be taken.

Chapter 8

When in France

LAETITIA DE WARREN
Laetitia de Warren is a French journalist and broadcaster, co-author of *Setting Up In France*, published by Merehurst.

Buying a house in a foreign community has far more human and social implications than one usually bargains for, even if the idea is simply to go there for a few weeks each year. However much you may wish for peace and quiet, you will hardly be living in splendid isolation. Acquiring a property in France means meeting the French and, from the very start, meeting them on a professional basis, because you will inevitably be dealing with the various boards and bodies that govern everyday life in any community - from the water board to the bank manager. You will, therefore, have to start by complying with the rules and habits of your new neighbours in those very areas of human contact that reveal people at their most annoying and absurd, because you will be meeting many of them in a formal and administrative context rather than a social one.

It is only after you have cut through the red tape that you can start adding your own personal touch, exerting your own influence in your relationship with the people around you. So, whether you only go to France on holiday, or whether you intend to settle there, the more practical knowledge you have of dealing with the system, the easier it will be to adapt yourself to it and subsequently make it suit your requirements.

PRACTICALITIES

Insuring your new home

Having gone through all the hassle of buying a property in France, the first move for the new owner is to protect his investment. The minute the final contract is signed, it is essential to take out adequate insurance. If your British insurance company has agents or offices in France, you may prefer to take out a policy with them. This does not mean, however, that you will be taking out a British policy – it will, in fact, be a French one, since this is the only type currently valid in France. The Single European Market is bringing in changes at a rate of knots, but these are EC knots, which means that it will be several years before we can hope to benefit from a common European insurance policy.

This being the case, you would be well advised, when dealing with a British-based insurance company, to ask for a detailed description of the policy covering your French property. Don't just assume that because you are using the same company you will be getting the same policy as the one you already have on your home in Britain. You need to know, for instance, what steps to take if you want to cancel the policy. It is often a longer and more complicated process in France than in Britain. You, as the policy-holder, have to follow a set procedure involving registered post and formal notifications. Make sure, therefore, that it has all been made clear to you beforehand. Indemnity is not calculated on the same basis, so do not wait to be faced with theft or damage before finding out on what terms you can hope to be compensated.

House insurance is not compulsory in France. However, it is strongly advisable, especially in the case of a holiday home that may lie empty for months or else be let to strangers. If you have bought a property that was formerly occupied and not just an empty shell you may find it simpler, at least to start with, to take over the vendor's insurance. This does not automatically expire with the sale of the house, unless the vendor has actually cancelled it. This generally means giving his insurance company or broker three months' advance warning by registered post, and he would certainly avoid taking such a definite measure before the final contract was signed. So the policy should continue to be valid for some time. It is vital, however, to have it officially transferred to your name; failure to do this could lead to predictable complications in the event of your having to make a claim.

Whatever policy you take out, whether with a French or a British company, make sure it covers, at minimum, fire, theft, flood, natural disaster and third party liability. However, you may feel more secure taking out a comprehensive policy (*assurances multirisques*). If the house is going to be empty part of the time, premiums will probably be higher than for a main residence. This additional cost could be offset if you decide to forgo contents insurance, having chosen to place inexpensive furniture and fittings in your French home. Even so, the insurance company may ask you to take particular safety measures such as extra locks, shutters, iron gratings on certain windows etc, especially in 'high risk' areas, which they themselves identify.

One important point to establish from the outset is the amount of time you have in which to file your claim. In France, this usually has to be done between two and five days after the incident which prompted the claim. If you do not live in your French property permanently you must make sure there is somebody in a position to let you know quickly of any problems. They will also have to warn the police in cases of criminal damage (theft, vandalism etc), because the official police statement is the incontrovertible evidence on which you will base your claim. An insurance company cannot dispute the police statement; so somebody must have the authority to go to the police station in your absence and report what has happened on your behalf. They may even have to get the police over to your house if the situation warrants it.

On a less dramatic note, you may simply need someone to mow your lawn once in a while or switch on the heating system before you arrive. There are several instances of British couples living in France who have set up as caretakers, looking after a number of holiday homes. There are also a few French associations who offer this kind of service, sometimes with a view to providing employment for young people. Whether they are French or British, professional caretakers will in all probability have made themselves known to the local authorities, so you can always try the nearest *mairie* for possible names and addresses.

In most cases, however, people tend to come to some sort of agreement with a neighbour who used to do the same for the previous owner. He may agree to keep an eye on the house in exchange for a modest fee or sometimes for a return favour, such as your allowing his horses or cows to graze on part of your land. A word of warning here: beware of an agreement involving the presence of someone else's animals on your property. You may suddenly discover on the day you wish to make use of the land that you cannot have the animals removed without the owner's agreement. So it might be a good idea to consult a *notaire* before doing anything, and in any case you should have the agreement set down in writing.

What a caretaker cannot normally do is pay your gas, electricity or water bills for you. That should be taken care of by a French bank where you should already have opened an account. You can have the bills paid by direct debit or standing order.

MAKING THE RIGHT CONNECTIONS

Water

Facing the problem of how to pay for water, electricity and gas obviously means that you have already sorted out the question of installing the supplies themselves. In some older properties these facilities may not already be available.

Naturally, you cannot have a house without water – this is just as true in France as elsewhere. If you are buying a property which has been inhabited at one time, even if it has been empty for years, there will be some form of water supply. Many British people, however, are attracted by old barns, while a few may wish to buy a piece of land and build on it. In both these cases, water may not automatically be supplied, so it is vital to know how you can gain access to it.

If your property is in or near an inhabited area, you will probably be able to establish a connection with the mains water system. This can be done with the help of the local *mairie* and the local water board. You would be well advised to find out as much as you can about water and electricity connections before coming to any final decision concerning the property. For example, the local authorities are under no obligation to connect your property to the water mains if it is isolated (in villages the supply will normally exist already). If they do establish the connection, there is every chance that you will have to pay for it – and it is expensive. In some cases, the *mairie* may be willing to take on part of the expense because, for instance, you are going to set up some form of activity that will be profitable to the locality as a whole, but don't count on it (see also page 126).

When there is a water main, the connection will often be made only to the edge of your property; the rest is up to you. So if you happen to have a well in working order or a spring on your property, do not eliminate the possibility of using that rather than the community network. If this is the case, make sure the water is safe to drink; have it analysed by the public health department. If in doubt, contact the *mairie* or the *DASS* (*Département de l'Action Sanitaire et Sociale*). This is particularly important in the south and in times of drought, when the water level is low and the risk of pollution high. You also need to make sure that there is no neighbourhood dispute as to the ownership of the spring. In any case, if this spring or well happens to be a source of water supply for other properties, you will not be allowed to cut it off.

If you are connected to the local network, your water consumption will be metered. The price of water varies considerably from region to region: it can be as much as ten times higher in some areas than others, depending on the availability of water. On average, it is more expensive than in Britain. France is a large country and there is a lot of structural work involved in building and maintaining an efficient network.

So when you fall in love with that picturesque, inexpensive barn in the middle of nowhere, don't forget that little details like water connection can suddenly make a huge difference to the overall price!

Electricity

In France, electricity is supplied by *EDF* (*Electricité de France*), the national public authority. There are still quite a number of houses (not necessarily in isolated areas) that are not wired, as they have not been lived in for some time. Whatever the case, it is always a good idea to ask a local representative of the electricity board to come and take a look at the house. He will be able to check that the wiring is up to standard. If you are having the house wired or re-wired, you must obtain a standards certificate or *certificat de conformité* stamped by the Electricity Users' Safety Commission or *CONSUEL*. A professional builder or electrician will see to that.

The running costs will vary according to the extent and power of your electrical system. If you intend to use powerful electrical appliances such as a washing machine or a cooker, you will need a power supply of at least 6 kW - probably more if you insist on taking your trusty British kettle, which, speaking from personal experience, is more than a match for the average French electricity supply!

The *EDF* representative will probably offer you a choice of several rates. There is, for instance, a 'seasonal' rate, which means that you will be charged the maximum tariff for some 30 days a year (normally in the winter) and the minimum rate the rest of the time. It will be up to you to control your electricity consumption during the 'peak' period - and do check the dates, since they may not fall on 30 consecutive days. You are warned beforehand when the maximum tariff is to be applied. For somebody who owns a holiday home and therefore tends to be there more often during the summer when the minimum rate is in operation, it may be an option worth considering.

As electricity in France is nuclear-powered, it is generally one of the less expensive sources of energy. More and more people are, therefore, turning to electricity when installing their heating system (see also page 129).

Gas

When consumers in France decide to choose gas for their heating it is usually because they are able to be connected to the mains network. This is normally the case in towns (which explains why mains gas is called *gaz de ville*), but gas is not so widely available in the country. If you wish to be linked to the network, you will have to pay for the connection - several hundred pounds in most cases. The work will be controlled by the gas board (*Gaz de France*), who will also install the meter. Gas bills are usually issued every four months.

If your house is not permanently occupied you must make sure that the various meters (gas, water and electricity) are accessible to the agents who come to read them. If they cannot gain access, you will be charged a lump sum based on your previous bills; you will then have to set about proving that you were not in the house at the time, and did not consume any energy during that particular period - a rather annoying waste of time, money and your own energy, if not that of your house!

If you cannot get connected to the mains network, you can have a gas tank installed in your property. You would need to check how this would affect your insurance premiums. Some gas suppliers are happy to install your tank free of charge if you agree to receive your supplies from them. You will have to sign a contract to this effect.

Insulation

How you insulate your property is naturally up to you, and has nothing to do with the French authorities, local or national. However, they are always keen to encourage better house insulation as a means of saving energy. The French agency for energy control (*L'Agence Nationale pour la Maîtrise de L'Energie*) will provide a thermal check-up (*diagnostic thermique*) for a fee. One of the agency's local representatives will come to your house and examine all the factors involved, such as the thickness of the walls, the size and number of windows, the exposure of the rooms, the existing equipment etc. All this information, along with your proposed budget, will then be fed into a computer and a solution which aims to meet your needs, means and wishes will be worked out. The report will include a scale of prices, useful for comparing with the actual estimates offered by heating engineers.

Telephone, fax and television

French Telecom (*France Télécom*) is a state-owned company. It is in the process of being separated from the Post Office, with the intention of making it even more efficient and competitive. Having a telephone installed is normally quite a painless procedure: you simply contact the local Telecom agency, and arrange for an engineer to come out, usually within 48 hours. If you are taking over an existing line, it is very quick and inexpensive. If you are having a new line installed and live in an isolated spot, it may take a few days more and will cost you around FF200.

If you want to have several telephone points put in, be sure to let the agency know beforehand. The engineer may not have enough spares with him if he is only told when he arrives, and it is not so easy to get him to come back.

Telephone bills are issued every two months. You will be offered the option of receiving a detailed bill, listing every telephone call, its length and cost. This can come in very useful if you intend to let the house or if there will be people staying there in your absence. You will know the exact number of telephone calls your tenants or guests have made, which can avoid a lot of conflict. This service will cost you a subscription fee of some FF20 every two months.

Another service available in France is the *Minitel*. This is a small telephone computer terminal which you can rent for as little as FF80 from French Telecom; it contains all sorts of information, such as the telephone directory for the whole of France, train or plane fares and times, theatre bookings, games etc.

Fax machines are easily obtainable but on the whole tend to be more expensive than in Britain, unless you can buy one as a company or a trader through commercial networks. If you bring over your own fax, it may need to be adapted, depending on the make or degree of sophistication. The manufactuers should be able to give you more specific information.

British car telephones do not work in France as the wavelength is different. This also goes for colour television. Unless you have a set that can be adapted to the French Secam system, there is not much point in bringing it with you. The same thing applies to video machines.

The licence for a colour television costs from FF580 a year. Satellite and cable television are more and more widespread; cable television is now available in practically all large towns in France. Satellite dishes are springing up all over the place, although they are still quite expensive to install (usually several thousand pounds).

HOME FROM HOME

Those many British nationals who have decided to take up permanent residence in France must sort out a series of practical problems, such as moving house, obtaining French documents, deciding whether they should take their car, finding schools for their children etc, as well as adapting to a new way of life, a new language and different habits. Spending three weeks in a French holiday resort, or even in one's own French holiday home, is all very well; settling in France once and for all implies a certain amount of organisation and a hefty dose of optimism.

The basic rule to remember in any situation is that in France everything always starts out by being complicated. This is because in every aspect of life, everything tends to be laid down in writing, and that being so, it is assumed that everybody must know about it. *'Nul n'est censé ignorer la loi*' – 'ignorance of the law is no excuse' – is one of the favourite maxims of the French, the civil code being the Frenchman's equivalent of the Gideon Bible. The resulting red tape can be extremely confusing to the uninitiated.

The secret for coping with the French administrative system is to stick to the letter of the law and avoid personal initiative. If, for instance, you have forgotten to put in the doctor's prescription when you sent your claim form to the social security office there is absolutely no point in going along and giving them the prescription: they will not take it. You must wait for them to send you back the whole wad of documents, informing you that you have forgotten the prescription. You can then send the complete file back. The waste of time and money for everybody is obvious to the meanest intelligence, but rules are rules. (This probably explains at least part of the financial deficit of the health-care system in France!)

Residence and removal documents

If you are an EC national, you will not need a work permit in France. The right to work there is included in your *carte de séjour* which will be your essential identification document on French territory. There are two ways of obtaining this.

The simplest thing is to obtain one when in France. You need to go to the *mairie* or nearest *préfecture* and ask if the *préfet*, who represents central government in each of the *départements* of France, is willing to deliver the *carte de séjour*. If he agrees, you can apply for one, producing your passport and proof of residence in France – either a copy of the lease if you are renting, or a copy of your final contract if you are a home-owner. Should the contract be too bulky or if you do not want to risk losing it you can ask the *notaire* who witnessed the sale to provide you with a certificate of acquisition (*attestation d'acquisition*). You will also need some passport format photos. Any payment required will be in the form of a fiscal stamp (*timbre fiscal*). These stamps have to be bought at a tobacconist's for the exact amount required; there is no point in arriving at the *préfecture* waving cheques or even bank-notes about: they won't be accepted. So make sure you find out beforehand whether you will need a *timbre fiscal* and for what amount. It may take you a while to find one: tobacconists always seem to have run out of the very stamp you need.

The second way is to obtain your papers in Britain, which means starting official proceedings at the very least six weeks before you move to France. You go to the French Consulate nearest your British residence and apply for a long-stay visa or *visa de longue durée*. In addition to several photographs and some form of identification, you will have to prove that you have a place of residence and a means of financial support in France (for example, a contract of employment). Once you have the visa, you take it to the *préfecture* in France and exchange it for the *carte de séjour.*

You must also provide an inventory, in French, of the personal household belongings that you are taking to France. Since April 1990, you no longer have to declare that you have been the owner of these items for more than three months, as was formerly the case (EC directive 89/604). However, you are only allowed to take over goods which you have already used. By the same token, you are now entitled to dispose of your belongings as you see fit from the moment they arrive in France (whereas until April 1990, you were not allowed to sell them for at least a year). However, these new measures do not apply to motor vehicles, mobile homes, boats or private planes, which are still subject to the 12-month sale ban.

As for the inventory, you no longer have to give details of the value of each item, as previously. This means that you do not need to fill in an official declaration known as CERFA/30/1584, or 'Statement of Importation', unless you are bringing motor vehicles, boats or planes, precious artefacts, collectors' items or weapons into France. These measures now also apply to goods and furniture destined for holiday homes.

For people who will not be earning their living in France – such as students or pensioners – the rules are being reviewed. For the moment, these people still have to produce a letter from their bank detailing their annual income, proof of residence in France witnessed by the local chief of police or the *maire*, as well as a certificate witnessed by a commissioner of oaths declaring that they have not been convicted for a criminal offence or made bankrupt. However, the European Council is now studying a series of directives intended to provide a right of residence throughout the Community for 'non-economically active persons', such as students and pensioners. This should lead to less red tape for those involved, and should take effect in the near future.

The French Consulate is not the only organisation to contact when it comes to moving your furniture. You must also get permission from the customs. You can use a customs agent who is familiar with this kind of problem, or simply go to the customs office nearest your future place of residence. Customs offices are usually to be found on, or near, industrial estates. They will want copies of your inventory and proof of your future residence in France. However, French customs officials are not always keen to deal with private individuals when it comes to removals, so you may be well advised to use an agent or a removal company.

If you do employ a removal company they too will need an inventory in French and a copy of your change of residence certificate, as they will be handling the paperwork. There are several firms specialising in removals to European countries. Using one of them will obviously avoid a lot of hassle, though there is no denying that it is an expensive operation.

Once you are in France, you can drive for a year on your British driving licence. You must then go to the *préfecture* or *sous-préfecture* (*Préfecture de Police* in Paris) with your *carte de séjour*, and you will be issued with a French licence. Again, you will need photographs. If you return to live in Britain, you will be given back your British licence. If you have brought over your own car you will need to get a *carte grise* (the equivalent of a car registration document) and change your number plates. Here again, the place to start is the *préfecture*. (Remember: you do not go to the *mairie* for anything to do with your car, however ubiquitous that public institution may be!)

Animals

Domestic animals may enter France provided they are vaccinated, in particular against rabies. They also have to be at least three months old. You will need to have your animal vaccinated in Britain by a veterinary surgeon registered with the Ministry of Agriculture who will provide you with an anti-rabies certificate. You will also need a health certificate, to be issued no sooner than five days before the animal leaves Britain. Dogs must also be vaccinated against distemper and hard-pad; with cats, it is feline gastro-entiritis and typhus. When the animal is in France, it must have an anti-rabies booster once a year.

You will find that the people to whom you actually have to show these documents are the British border police at ports or airports. In general, French customs seem to have a rather relaxed attitude to incoming domestic animals. However, it would be very unwise to rely on their lack of interest and to avoid bothering about the proper certificates. Provided you can get past the British border police – which is doubtful – you may get to France on the very day when French customs officials are staging a crackdown on illicit animal importation. The next thing you know is that your animal is back on a ship or plane to Britain, where it will automatically be refused entry, unless you agree to have it put in quarantine and to pay a hefty fine. You may even end up with a prison sentence.

In France, you will notice lots of dogs and cats with a number tattooed on one of their ears. This is not compulsory, but many pet owners take the precaution, which can come in useful if the animal gets lost. Each individual number is logged, together with the owner's name and address, into a central computer, controlled by the *Société Protectrice des Animaux*, the French equivalent of the RSPCA. When people find an animal with a tattooed ear, they usually take it immediately to one of the *SPA* centres, which will be able to track down the owner thanks to that individual number. The owner himself has a special certificate with all the animal's details and the number, which he receives from the vet when the animal is tattooed. It is a perfectly harmless operation, but quite expensive: about FF700.

Health

Temporary visitors

Even if you go over to your holiday home in France for only a few weeks each year, you should take some precautions in case of health problems or accident. You should go to your local Department of Health office to obtain form E111, which covers medical care for Common Market nationals. If you need to see a doctor in France, get him to sign this form; it will entitle you to reimbursement when you go back to Britain, because in France you will have to pay for your visit. If you have to go to hospital, you may be asked to pay in advance, even at the equivalent of a National Health Service institution (*Hôpital Conventionné*). To avoid this, ask the DH for a second form, form E112; this covers what the French call *La prise en charge*, ie actual hospitalisation.

As an added precaution, a temporary insurance of the Europ Assistance type is definitely advisable, especially if you are travelling around. These schemes normally offer all sorts of facilities, including prompt repatriation in case of emergency. Some even provide a lawyer if you get clapped into prison for any reason.

Permanent residence

Your first move before leaving Britain is to contact the overseas branch of the DH at Newcastle upon Tyne and ask them to send you their various brochures on the system in France and how it applies to you. As a member of the EC, you are entitled to the same health service as the French. This applies to employees or self-employed people who have paid British National Insurance as well as to State pensioners and, finally, to the children or dependants of all these people.

If you are a pensioner, there is nothing to stop you receiving your pension from Britain, either directly, or by bank transfer. You can also, if you wish, ask for it to be transferred to an account in Britain.

In France, medical care is usually paid for and the sum then reimbursed. When you go to see a doctor, he will sign a social security form; if he gives you a prescription, you take it to a chemist, who will also fill in the form. You must pay him for the medicine. You then send the completed form to your local social security office. This will ensure the reimbursement of the full cost of the medicine, and 70–80 per cent of the doctor's fee, provided he is *conventionné*, ie that he has signed the social security convention. If a doctor, or a clinic for that matter, is not *conventionné*, you will not be reimbursed.

If you want to benefit from the French social security system, you must obtain a card and a number from your local social security office, just as you would in Britain for National Insurance. This is also the office where you apply for reimbursement. In the case of very expensive treatment, the doctor or hospital will often provide you with a special form, which enables you to ask for a preliminary agreement from the health service. This agreement means you will not have to pay for the treatment, provided you produce your social security card on the day. It is advisable to send the agreement form to the health service by registered post. They have a fortnight in which to answer; if they do not, it is considered that they have agreed. It is always better to have proof that you sent the form on a given date, in case there is a dispute later on.

You are free to choose your own GP as well as a medical specialist, wherever you or he may live. You need a prescription from your GP to get the help of a nurse, a physiotherapist or any other medical auxiliary, otherwise the fees you pay them will not be reimbursed.

Alternatively - or, indeed, additionally - a well-known British private medical insurance company provides cover for expatriates. This includes full cover for hospital accommodation, specialist fees and all forms of treatment, as well as out-patient consultations. It also covers evacuation back to Britain. The fees for medical cover, payable quarterly, are as follows: £29 if you are under the age of 21; £87 between 21 and 49; £127 between 50 and 64. The evacuation cover is an optional extra.

Driving

On French roads, the speed limit is 130km an hour on motorways; 110km an hour on dual carriageways; 90km an hour on ordinary roads; 50 or 60km an hour in built-up areas or *agglomérations*; and 45km an hour in city centres.

The legal limit for the level of alcohol in the bloodstream is 0.8 grams per litre. Drinking and driving is punishable by a prison sentence of between two months and two years and a fine of up to FF30,000. There are random breath tests – so even if you have committed no offence, you can be stopped by the police and breathalysed, especially during the great holiday migrations. Should they feel that you are not in a fit state to drive, the police are also entitled to make you leave your car on the spot and continue your journey on foot.

If you are stopped for speeding, you will often be asked to pay your fine there and then, especially if you are driving a car with foreign number plates. It is the simplest way for the authorities to make sure that foreign drivers pay their fines and do not disappear into the blue in the hope that nobody will be bothered to pursue the affair any further.

There are also radar speed traps, sometimes equipped with cameras. The motorists who are caught speeding receive an official letter after several weeks, informing them that on such a day, at such a time, in such a place, they were exceeding the speed limit by so many kilometres an hour, and politely ordering them to go to their nearest police station and leave their driving licence there for a given period of time.

Finally, do not forget that there are tolls on French motorways. If you have no cash, you can pay by credit card.

Rail travel

If all this has put you off driving in France, try taking a train. The French railway system, or *SNCF*, is generally clean, modern and efficient. There are more and more high-speed trains that put towns like Lyons within two hours and Rennes within one and a half hours of Paris. There are a number of reductions in train fares for pensioners, students and families.

Schools

A major question for British families settling in France is that of their children's education. Apart from the *Lycée International* at St Germain-en-Laye near Paris and *L'Ecole Bilingue* in the French capital, there are virtually no English educational facilities in France. A lot of British parents choose the best of both worlds and start by enrolling their children in French nursery and primary schools so that they get a good lasting knowledge of the language, and then send them to a boarding school in Britain.

French children start school at the age of six. Before that, they practically all go to nursery school from the age of three, or even two. Those whose mothers work outside the home can go to a municipal crèche from a very early age – six months, in some cases. As usual, there are never enough crèches to accommodate all the children, and French parents complain bitterly about it. At least they do exist, which is not the case in all European countries (which shall remain nameless!). In nursery schools – either private fee-paying or State-owned free schools – children are involved in creative activities, and learn personal hygiene as well as some basic reading, writing and sums.

Once the children start primary school, be it private (*école privée*) or State-run (*école publique*), they enter the French school system, which means the same syllabus and the same major exams throughout the country. Primary school lasts five years from *CP* (*cycle préparatoire*), through *CE1* (*cycle élémentaire 1*), *CE2* (*cycle élémentaire 2*), *CM1* (*cycle moyen 1*) up to *CM2* (*cycle moyen 2*).

When starting secondary school, children who do not attend a private establishment go to either a *collège* or a *lycée*, depending on what is available in their neighbourhood. The first year in secondary school is known as *sixième*, or sixth. The numbering of classes in France is then in reverse order from that in Britain, from *sixième* to *première*, with the final year being called *terminale*; in other words, it is a countdown towards the end of school.

The collège will take pupils up to and including *troisième*. The *lycée* will take them to the end of their school studies and the final exam, the *baccalauréat*. So children who go to *collège* will, after *troisième*, go to a *lycée* at the age of 14 or 15; there, they will either prepare a *baccalauréat* (literary, scientific, mathematical, technical or technological), a technical diploma (*brevet technique*), a vocational one (*brevet professionnel*) or a vocational training certificate (*certificat d'aptitude professionnel*). All this will depend on their own capability, their preferences, the advice of their teachers etc.

After secondary school, young people have the choice between a 'vocational' or a 'selective' system. The 'vocational' option takes them to university straight after they have passed the *baccalauréat*. They then work towards specific degrees, which are obtained after a varying number of years, and which correspond to the BA, MA, PhD etc in Britain. This system applies to most subjects, including medicine, law, economic sciences, languages and literature.

The 'selective' system requires at least one preliminary exam, if not two, on top of the *baccalauréat*. It applies to other specialised subjects, and leads to the famous *grandes écoles*, of which the French are so proud. These are the institutions that are considered as forming the élite of France – the scientists, engineers, administrators, teachers, politicians and businessmen who lead the affairs of the country. The system has undeniable advantages for those who succeed in it; whether it has as many advantages for the country as a whole is another question.

British first-year students who wish to attend a university in France must obtain a *demande d'admission* (admission request) from the cultural services of the French Embassy in London. Students in other years must apply directly to the university of their choice in France. There are grants for foreign students: once again, details are obtainable from the French Embassy.

Students who are looking for a place to stay can obtain advice and information from the *Centre Régional des Oeuvres Universitaires et Scolaires* (*CROUS*) in Paris.

Chapter 9
Planning and Renovation

ANNE HILL
Anne Hill is a teacher of languages and a regular visitor to France, where she spends several months each year researching and renovating a derelict property.

If you are intending to buy a property in France or have already bought one, it is quite likely that it will need attention to bring it to the standard required. There are countless stories of people finding dream homes – the eighteenth-century barn located in an idyllic setting at a giveaway price, for example. While such properties do exist, they are quite likely to come without running water, sanitation, electricity, a roof and much else. In reality, the cost of getting such a property to the most basic level of habitation can be several times the purchase price. What also has to be included in the equation is the time, energy and commitment involved in restoring a property.

A willingness to take on a property requiring extensive work has several advantages:

- It gives you a far wider range of properties to consider. In parts of rural France there are large numbers of unoccupied properties, often in a derelict state.
- Because such properties are considerably cheaper than those in good condition, it makes buying a property in France possible, even if you have very limited means.
- A range of buildings which, by their very nature, will require major changes to turn into homes are an added option for you – for example, barns, cowsheds, mills, bakeries, shops and schools.

However, before taking on the commitment of a property which will need extensive renovation (*une propriété à restaurer* or even *une propriété en ruines*) it is worth carrying out some self-evaluation to decide whether such a project is right for you. If you have a great deal of money available for the project you can pay not only for other people to carry out the work, but for someone else to supervise the renovation. The following section is intended rather for people who propose:

- to carry out all the work themselves;
- personally to choose, employ and supervise others to carry out the work;
- to do some work themselves and employ others for selected tasks.

It may seem that employing other people to carry out the renovation relieves you of the work. In reality it demands time, attention and organisation.

If you are planning to settle in France, then you have more time at your disposal, but if your visits are limited to holidays only, then the following points need careful consideration.

Self-assessment

How do you like to spend your holidays and leisure time?
Do you enjoy taking part in some form of activity – sport, outdoor pursuits, leisure activities with a specific objective? Or do you prefer a more leisurely approach with the emphasis on relaxation, unwinding through doing as little as possible, as slowly as possible? Becoming involved in house renovation – particularly at a distance – can be a demanding and at times stressful undertaking, so you need to be fairly confident that you can incorporate it into your concept of how holiday and leisure time should be spent. As long as you find it an interesting and worthwhile way to spend your leisure time, everything is fine. If, however, it becomes a chore and yet another responsibility, you will return from your time in France feeling tired and in need of a holiday.

How good are your DIY skills?
Is your experience limited to a spot of straightforward decoration or have you already carried out a major project on your home in the UK? There is no reason why someone with very little previous experience could not buy a property for renovation in France. However, you would have to be willing to acquire new skills and knowledge and you would soon come to realise that learning by your mistakes can be costly and upsetting when it is a question of your home. Even if you intend employing others to do the work, it makes sense:

- to know precisely what you want done;
- to understand how the work is carried out;
- to be aware of what materials will be used;
- to have an appreciation of the time and effort involved.

If you intend to carry out work on the property yourself and already have DIY experience, you may still find that the renovation work necessary demands knowledge and skills outside your experience. You will probably also need to acquire these and be prepared to 'learn on the spot'. However, your previous experience of DIY will be of value in making you aware of how much time, frustration and drudgery are involved in completing the tasks. If you have already handled a major project – building an extension or installing a bathroom, for example – and seen it through from conception to completion, then you will have confidence in your own ability to do it again.

How much time do you have available?

It makes sense to work out how much time each year you intend to spend in France. What is your annual leave entitlement? Is it possible to take most of it in one 'lump' or are you expected to take it in shorter amounts? Is it realistic to plan to spend all your holiday time at your property or will other commitments (visiting relatives, involvement in your local community in the UK, your children's social activities) make this unrealistic? Certain major renovation projects need to be completed once started – installing new French windows, for example – so you must have an assured length of time available if you are doing the job yourself.

If your job gives you more flexibility in arranging your work and leisure time (freelance workers) or you have longer than average holidays (teachers, lecturers) then you will be able to spend more time at your property and get tasks completed more quickly. If you have limited amounts of time and money and are working on a property which needs major renovation for just two to three weeks a year, the number of years it would take to complete your work could stretch into double figures.

Do you have access to help?

There are many occasions when an extra pair of hands (or more) proves invaluable. Are you buying a property alone, with a partner or as a group? Even if you plan to employ someone to carry out the major jobs, there will still be times when you need help or advice or both. Start thinking of people willing to devote some time and labour to your project. Student acquaintances might find the offer of free board and accommodation in return for their services a very attractive proposition. Will you have neighbours at your French property? Although you cannot assume that they will offer help, they will almost certainly be glad to offer advice. This could be particularly useful if they have already worked or had work done on their property and you can gain from their experience. Assuming that your neighbours are French, a shared interest like this can be a natural and practical way of getting acquainted and starting to become part of your new community.

How good are your language skills?

Undertaking renovation work involves a good deal of contact with local tradespeople, officials and workers, and you cannot assume that everyone you deal with is going to speak and understand English. While you may be proficient at ordering meals in a restaurant and buying fruit at the local market, would you be able to:

- explain precisely what size and type of wood you require in a timber yard where there is no convenient list of goods and prices to point to, and the noise of various machines at work is making conversation difficult anyway?
- make a phone call from a noisy bar to the local plumber due at your property in an hour's time to explain that you will be delayed because your car has broken down and to ask if he could call tomorrow instead?

These may seem extreme examples, but to cope with a variety of situations you will need a reasonable level of comprehension of everyday spoken French and the basic knowledge and confidence to get your message across clearly and appropriately. Much of the vocabulary you will use is new and specialised. This need not be a problem provided you are reasonably proficient at general conversation, and make sure you have any questions you want to ask prepared in advance and a dictionary to hand to bale you out in tricky situations.

If you feel your French needs some improvement, then classes or personal tuition in the UK could be time and money well spent if they enable you to carry out your work in France with greater ease. Try contacting your local Adult Education Institute or look for someone who gives private tuition. In either case, explain:

- precisely why you are taking classes;
- which skills you wish to improve (speaking and understanding spoken French);
- which areas of vocabulary and phrases you need to acquire.

How patient are you?

Are you prepared to wait several years before your property is halfway habitable or do you get impatient if tasks are not completed in a few weeks? However much enthusiasm, energy and pre-planning you take over the Channel to your property with each visit, there are quite likely to be delays and setbacks. For example, the materials you need are out of stock and will not be available until after the holidays; or the local builder booked to replace your windows can no longer do the work at the times you require because he is ill. Incidents like this could mean that the job cannot be done until your next visit, which may not be for another six months, or that other work to be done on the property can no longer be carried out because it can only be started on completion of the original task.

Would this sort of experience frustrate you to the point of spoiling your holiday? Or could you adopt a philosophical approach to the situation and still feel your trip had been enjoyable?

Tackling the work

Even though the property you buy may be in poor condition, you will no doubt feel it has great potential and quickly build up a picture in your mind of how it will look when restored. Before this picture becomes too fixed, it is worth keeping an open mind and looking at other dwellings in the locality. There are usually sound reasons for particular features – small windows to keep out the sun, living accommodation on the first floor to avoid dampness. By observing and talking to local people you may discover important points to bear in mind before planning major changes. Perhaps you intend to employ an architect to draw up plans. It is still worth conducting your own enquiries and taking the time and trouble to look at other properties, particularly those which have been restored to a good standard and in a way that is in keeping with the local community and architecture.

It is useful to look closely at what materials are predominantly used for construction in your locality – tiles, slate, wood, brick, stone or rendering? Use of one material in preference to another can be for a very good reason:

- stone quarried locally is cheap and readily available;
- wood felled in forests nearby provides a large supply of cheap material;
- tiles for roofing may be well suited to the climate and the environment.

At some stage you need to draw up a list of the work to be done and decide in what order to tackle the tasks. You may decide to call in experts to help you assess what jobs should be done – for example, to check the state of your woodwork. It may be very obvious, even to an untrained eye, what needs doing, such as being able to see daylight through your roof or dangerous flooring. When compiling your list of tasks, make sure that there is a progression so that the completion of one job enables you to start the next. Assuming that you are starting from scratch, your list could be something like this:

- roof
- electricity
- flooring
- water supply
- sanitation
- windows, doors
- interior repairs

Before embarking on any of these items, there are a number of people and organisations to contact.

The town hall (*l'Hôtel de ville* or *mairie*)

You will inevitably be in contact with your local town hall, if only to pay your rates. If you are planning any major changes it is the place to go to find out what you can and cannot do.

People who are interested in buying a property to convert into a home – such as a barn or farm building – should contact the local town hall to see if this is allowed. Permission is not always given automatically, particularly in a conservation area (*un site protégé* or *un quartier protégé*), so check before you go ahead with the purchase.

Whatever type of property you are buying, if it is in a conservation area stringent rules and regulations for the protection of the area (*la protection des monuments naturels et des sites*) will affect what changes can be made. Permission for changes or even repair of existing features has to be sought from *l'Architecte des Bâtiments de France.*

If you know how you intend to carry out all your work and have drawn up plans for the whole of your renovation project, these need to be submitted to the mayor so that you can apply for the appropriate permission (*un permis de construire*). However, if you intend to carry out the improvements over a period, perhaps tackling one or two major jobs each year, you may not have a clear picture of what you intend to do in the long term. In this case you can apply for permission to carry out one specific task initially (*déclaration de travaux exempte de permis de construire* or *déclaration de clôture*). Your application will still be subject to rigorous scrutiny and needs to follow the procedure set down. For example, if you were seeking permission to replace your roof, these are the stages the procedure might follow:

- Permission must be sought from the *Ministère de l'Equipement*, detailing precisely which materials you intend to use and any alterations (including windows) proposed.
- A *déclaration de travaux* would be made by your local town hall, stating your name and home address, what work you intend to do and where.
- A letter would be sent to you, informing you that the *déclaration de travaux* had been registered and that you must wait a set period (in this case two months) to see if there are objections (*notification du délai d'instruction*) before proceeding.
- Assuming that there are no objections you would receive a letter itemising the exact type of slate or tile to be used, stating that no changes can be made to the existing style, shape, angle or height (*prescriptions relatives à une déclaration de travaux*).

While the official procedures and regulations may seem daunting, the mayor or his representative may be able to ease your path through them and find a more human approach. This is one reason why it is important to pay a visit early on in the proceedings. It is advisable to approach him as an individual seeking advice and information from someone knowledgeable about the town or district, rather than with a list of what you intend to do. If you can assure him that you will carry out any works sensitively and in a way that will blend in with other buildings and help to enhance the local community and environment, then he may well prove to be a useful ally.

The water board

Any work involving water will mean contacting the local water board (*Syndicat de gestion des eaux*), whether it be to arrange for the connection of a water supply or alterations to an existing system. Information about existing water supplies and plans should be available at the town hall (see also page 107).

If your property has no existing water supply, an official from the water board will need to make a visit to inspect it and to work out its location in relation to the nearest water pipe. After this inspection you will receive a quotation (*un devis*) for the cost of connecting your property to the water supply. This quotation is only for the connection work and does not include the costs of digging any necessary channels for pipes (*terrassement non compris*). Digging channels is your responsibility, so you will need to decide whether to carry it out yourself or pay someone else to do it. The cost of this work will vary according to the distance from your property to the water supply and the type of land in which the channel has to be dug (for example, digging a channel in rock would be more costly than through ordinary soil).

Once the work is completed, the water board will connect you to the water supply and install a water meter. Water charges are levied according to how much water you use.

Although British plumbing fittings are all metric they are not the same size as French fittings (the diameter size is different). This means that it is difficult to match British and French fittings unless you are fairly skilful. It is worth considering this, therefore, before you decide to bring fittings out from the UK. If you did so and then discovered while working in France that you were missing an essential fitting, it would not be possible to buy it in France, and trying to accommodate the nearest French equivalent into your work could be difficult and time-consuming.

Sanitation

Before deciding to buy a property you need to find out whether there is an existing toilet. If not:

- Is your property in an area already served by a communal sewage system?
- What are the options for installing your own toilet?

Installing your own toilet and sewage system is likely to be costly and involve a lot of extra work. Before you embark on such a project, ask at the town hall if there is any possibility of a communal sewage system being installed in your village or area in the near future. If so, it could be worth your while to wait for this, using a chemical toilet in the meantime.

However, if you are in a remote village or away from other properties, you may well have to install a septic tank (*fosse septique*). It is useful to find out how other people in the area, especially immediate neighbours, have tackled the problem:

- What sort of tank have they used?
- Where have they sited it?
- How did they have it installed?
- Who did the installation?
- How much did this cost?
- How long did it take?

You can put it on your own land or it might be possible to put it on communal land, with the permission of the mayor. If neither option is possible, then it can be placed inside the dwelling as long as it is not in the living quarters (in a cellar, perhaps).

A local builder who has already carried out similar projects in your area will be able to give advice on ways of installing a septic tank and will be conversant with regulations and specifications. If you wish to make your own enquiries, contact:

- the town hall;
- *Direction Départementale de d'Equipement* (*DDE*);
- *Direction Départementale des Affaires Sanitaires et Sociales* (*DDASS*).

It is also worth asking at the town hall if the *département* publishes any handbook on sanitation (*guide de l'assainissement*).

The electricity board

To have electricity connected to your property or to make enquiries about an existing supply, contact your local branch of *Electricité de France/Gaz de France* (the two services are combined). They are primarily concerned with the electricity supply up to the point where it enters your property. While they will inspect an existing system and give advice if asked, this is considered your responsibility (see also page 109).

There are three types of electricity supply normally allocated for domestic use in France – 3kW, 6kW or 9kW. To help you choose which is most appropriate for your needs, *EDF/GDF* give the following guidelines:

- 3kW for lighting and domestic appliances such as television, fridge, vacuum cleaner, iron;
- 6kW for the above appliances plus water heater plus *one* of the following: washing machine, electric cooker or dishwasher;
- 9kW for the appliances listed for 6kW plus *two* of the following in use at the same time; washing machine, electric cooker or dishwasher.

In comparison with average consumption of electricity in the UK (where the normal domestic supply is 30 amps), these allowances may not seem adequate. Before coming to a decision, it is best to try and work out:

- exactly which electrical appliances you will have in your property;
- the kilowatt value of each appliance;
- which appliances you are likely to operate at the same time;
- the total kilowatt power you will need.

If your needs are likely to exceed these amounts, you should contact the electricity board to enquire about having a more powerful supply (9–36kW), which will be more expensive. An electric shower uses a lot of power so make sure to include this in your calculations if you plan to install one – even at a later date.

As voltage in France is the same as in the UK you can use electrical appliances from home in France. The sockets (*les prises*) and the plugs (*les fiches*) are different. If there is no existing electrical system in your property there is nothing to stop you installing a British system, using British materials and specifications. However, if you do this you would have to be certain that you brought everything necessary with you from the UK (imagine the frustration of not being able to continue with your work because of not having one small but crucial item). Problems could arise at a later date if you wanted to sell your property or even if a French electrician had to work on the system.

The point at which the internal electricity system starts is at the circuit breaker (*le disjoncteur*). This has the following functions:

- It enables you to cut off the electricity supply to your home, eg to carry out electrical work.
- It automatically cuts off the supply for safety reasons, such as in the case of a short circuit (*un court-circuit*).
- It fixes the maximum amount of power you can use. If you go over this it will cut off.

When buying electrical appliances in France the label *PROMETELEC* (*Association pour de développement et l'amélioration des installations intérieures*) indicates those which are safe and suited to your needs. For electrical materials, trade-marks which include the sign *NF* (*normes françaises*) will conform to the agreed French safety standards.

For further information concerning electricity supply or goods, ask at your local electricity board for a booklet (*Le livret de l'usager de l'électricité*) which is clearly set out and well illustrated.

Gas

Electricité de France/Gaz de France also deal with gas supply and connection. Gas supply is limited mainly to cities and towns; the use of bottled gas is very common, so if your property is in a rural area this might be the only option for you (see also page 109).

Getting organised

Once you start to accumulate information and documentation, it is a good idea to start a file. This could contain:

- addresses and phone numbers of town hall, electricity board etc, with names of contacts and opening times;
- addresses and phone numbers for useful shops and suppliers of materials with opening times and information on delivery service and charges;
- a list of public holidays;
- quotations;
- receipts for materials and work done.

As you embark on your preliminary enquiries and start work on your property, it can be very useful to keep a diary of your renovation work. This might include:

- what task you planned for each trip;
- how long you thought it would take;
- the materials used;
- the time each job actually took to complete (this can be helpful when planning future projects);
- cost of materials and labour.

Tools

Whether you intend to employ others to carry out renovation work or do it yourself, it is necessary to keep a set of basic tools at your property in France. If you already have a good range of tools, you will probably start by taking those with you. It is possible to manage with one set, but many people find it easier to buy duplicates of the most commonly used tools and leave those in France. Although this is costly, it avoids having to get together the items needed for each trip and will gain extra space in your car. It can become complicated when you start searching for a tool at your home in the UK and cannot decide whether or not it is in France. The solution is to keep an up-to-date inventory of your tool box in each home. On average, tools cost roughly the same in France as in the UK, so you will be able to buy anything you need while in France.

Suppliers

It is helpful to start compiling a list of shops and suppliers of tools and materials for DIY in advance of your needs. As well as keeping you abreast of events in your area, your local paper will carry advertisements from local shops and suppliers and keep you informed of special offers and sales. If you keep all information about the price of materials in your file, it can come in handy when working out costs of work and comparative prices of materials in the UK and France.

An obvious place to shop is the nearest DIY superstore. This will often be adjacent to the hypermarket in the local out-of-town shopping centre (*centre commercial*). Here you will be offered a wide selection of goods at competitive prices, plus additional services such as cutting of wood. Although you will find many of the items you require here, don't overlook the smaller shops and merchants. As in the UK, smaller concerns can often carry a wider range of supplies than large supermarkets, charge similar or cheaper prices for certain items and you are more likely to get useful advice on the best product to buy for your particular need.

If you are based in an agricultural area, another possible source for buying tools and materials could be your local market. It is possible to find good second-hand tools at low prices if you are prepared to search around. Any shops geared towards farmers (look for *agri-* or *agricole* in the names) are very likely to carry a range of general tools and supplies.

Hiring equipment

There will probably be some tools or items of equipment you do not wish to buy, either because they are too costly or because you will only need to use them once. It is possible to hire such items as ladders, cement mixers and sanders, but such services are not as widespread as in the UK, especially in some rural areas. To find a hire service, try looking in the yellow pages of the local phone directory, ask at the local DIY shop or look at the notice-board outside the hypermarket (look for names including *location* or *loco-*). As a general rule, it is more costly to hire such items in France.

Materials

For any work involving building materials – bricks, tiles, sand, cement etc – it is probably best to shop locally. Look for local builders' merchants or builders (*entreprise de bâtiments* or *entreprise de construction*) who sell materials. They will usually deliver goods, but will charge for this service. Check what the charge is before placing an order. You may find it is a set amount, regardless of how much you are buying. If so, it may be worth ensuring that you order everything you are likely to need for some time – though obviously not products with a limited shelf life, such as cement and plaster.

Transporting materials

Those planning to carry out work themselves or buy in materials for others to do the work will be continually transporting materials to and fro, so it is worth considering your form of transport. For most people it is not practical to change their existing car instantly to take account of this. If, however, you are planning a change of car, you might bear these requirements in mind. A hatchback or estate car will come in useful; a set of ladder bars is also an asset, as is a trailer. Even if you don't bring a trailer with you, it can be useful to have a tow bar fitted to your car. Many people in rural areas have trailers, especially on farms, and you may be able to negotiate the loan of one. You would need to check the insurance implications with regard to your green card.

For other items, such as electrical materials, paint and basic household tools, try the hardware shop (*quincaillerie*). Fairly general electric materials will also be found in most shops selling electrical goods (*électro-ménager*).

Wood can be bought in a DIY shop, but tends to be expensive for small amounts. If you need large amounts of wood, contact local builders' yards to see if they stock it. Look out for large timber yards attached to sawmills if you are in an area which is widely forested. These can be an excellent source of cheap wood, but do not always deliver.

With few exceptions, all the tools and materials required for renovation work are available in France. While it may initially seem easier to bring such items with you from home, it can be much simpler to buy what you need in France. It can save time, transport costs and, almost as important, bring custom to the shopkeepers and traders of your new community.

Builders

Many British people, having bought their property in France, will ask a builder from home to take charge of the renovation work for them. They may feel that communication with one of their compatriots will be easier, especially when discussing issues of a technical nature. However, you need to be careful. There are important considerations to bear in mind. In France, professional builders are registered and have to be covered by insurance. If any problems should arise for which the builder is responsible, he will be obliged to return and put it right. He can also be deemed responsible for the consequences of his work (for example, seepage from a faulty septic tank), which is why he is always insured.

Builders must guarantee their work for ten years, so if during that time they go out of business, you will still be covered by the insurance. In addition to this, employing local trades- and craftspeople is another way of making contacts in your new community and of contributing to its economy. If, however, you still prefer to employ an overseas builder, be sure, at the very least, to take out your own form of insurance policy (*assurance dommage-ouvrage*) to cover the work for ten years after its completion.

It may appear from the dos and don'ts and numerous words of caution that renovating a property in France is an onerous task, only undertaken by people looking for extra work and problems. While this is true, it can also bring many rewards, including:

- a home renovated to suit your needs and preferences;
- a chance to make contacts and become part of the community;
- a practical way of improving your French language skills;
- many work-filled, but enjoyable holidays in France.

Chapter 10
An Introduction to Setting Up in Business

NORMAN SMITH
Norman Smith is a British accountant, resident in France; he specialises in practical advice and assistance to private individuals and businesses in France.

It is important that you really know what you are letting yourself in for if you are thinking of living abroad, let alone setting up a business in a foreign country.

Bear in mind that it will be a culture shock; it is a completely different way of life – things are not done in the same way as in your own country. Living abroad is not the same thing as spending three or four weeks' holiday there. You have to immerse yourself in every way in the local life and accept the way things are done locally. You cannot expect to impose your own particular ways of doing things on people who have been doing them their way for generations and who think that their way is the best – particularly in France, where people are proud. The French believe – and in most cases I think they are correct – that their particular way of life is probably the best in the world. There may be an element of truth in this, and we should respect their opinion.

The next step should always be to consider what business you are going to run. Do you already have knowledge of running a business of any sort? Have you done it in your own country? Do you have business management experience, gained through working in a senior position for someone else? If you have none of these requirements, then perhaps you should think carefully before coming to France to set up independently. Local people know more about running businesses than strangers coming into an area.

Even if you have a general idea of the business you want to go into, or experience of being in business at home, the local conditions may be such that you need to relearn all about it. So you would be well advised to work for someone else initially, though not necessarily in the area of France where you would wish to set up, as there may be problems of competition later on. This would enable you to learn about local practices in the particular trade, and about business conditions in general.

When it comes to the nature of your business, consider whether it will involve dealing with the general public. Will the public accept you readily as a foreigner in this particular trade or service? It may well be an advantage to be a foreigner in some trades, but it could be a disadvantage in others. Take the question of names, for instance: if you want to gain local acceptance, you should avoid using foreign-sounding names for your business. Choose words that are either French or, at least, easy for the French to pronounce.

Remember that it will take you longer, as a foreigner, to be accepted; you will not necessarily be welcomed with open arms by the public or the local tradespeople. You need to communicate in business, so you must have at least a reasonable knowledge of spoken French. It is essential at least to be able to read French, because you will be flooded with official documents and you must be able to understand them. As time goes on, you must make the effort to learn to write French as well, if only so that you can reply to official mail. Even the smallest businesses receive enormous amounts of official correspondence: this has to be answered even if it means sending in a nil return. So you need a basic knowledge of French to be able to cope with it all.

If you are starting a new business, bear in mind the high failure rate of such enterprises everywhere in the world – and France is no exception. Some two-thirds of new businesses fail within the first two or three years. On a more positive note, remember that France is the home of small businesses, owing to the individuality of French people, who like doing things on their own or in small groups rather than being part of a large organisation. There are enormous numbers of small businesses in France; the economic philosophy accepts and encourages the idea of setting up small businesses of all sorts – craftsmen, shopkeepers, small manufacturing businesses, professional services, etc.

One way of setting up could be to take over an existing business. Many small businesses close each year because there is no one to take them over. There is a well-developed network in France of organisations which help businesses seeking someone to take them over, because the owner is retiring or for any other reasons; the information is available from Chambers of Commerce in particular, or from *Chambres des Métiers* who are listed in local telephone books. There is one in every large city.

Taking over an existing business has many advantages; however, beware of what you are buying. It is preferable to take over only the goodwill and perhaps some assets; avoid taking over liabilities, as you can rarely verify them.

Where should you go for advice?

In Britain, there are the Department of Trade and Industry, the French Industrial Development Board and the French Chamber of Commerce in London (although that is mainly intended for French businesses in Britain). However, the Chamber issues a magazine, *INFO*, which may be of interest. Doing business in France was featured in one particular issue (September 1989).

In France, you can go for information to the Franco-British Chamber of Commerce, in Paris. It has branches in many regional cities and is a good place for meeting people in Franco-British trade. There are also the British Consulates.

And then there is a whole network of French sources: French Chambers of Commerce in every big town, and *Chambres des Métiers* for artisans, as well as all the local government authorities who try to encourage businesses to set up in their area. The *communes*, the *départements* and the regions all have services to inform and encourage people who want to set up in business. The French statistical service, the INSEE, issues information, generally free of charge, on a regular basis and if you go along to their offices they are very helpful. Another organisation, ESPACE, is for people who want training in business.

Methods of business organisation

You need to decide whether you want the protection of limited liability. This will determine whether you should set up as a sole trader or create a limited liability company which will give you protection in the event that the business does not work out. But remember, it would only give limited protection because banks or suppliers may refuse to trade with a limited liability company, particularly a new one, if they do not know the people running it and are not aware of their business experience. They may require personal guarantees. So, there again, it may take a while for you to gain their confidence.

Limited liability company

If you wish to set up a limited liability company, the simplest form is called an SARL (*Société à Responsabilité Limitée*). Ninety per cent of all French limited companies are of this type (the others are *Sociétés Anonymes*): it is a traditional way of setting up small businesses. A declaration has to be filed with various government departments, and the company must be registered at the Register of Commerce and Corporations (*Registre de Commerce et des Sociétés*). Notice of the formation must also be made public. Some of the particular requirements for a limited liability company in France are more bureaucratic than in Britain, and more demanding; you have to produce more paperwork and fill in more forms in order to become registered.

An SARL needs a minimum capital of FF50,000, all of which has to be paid out in advance. Part of it can be introduced in goods, materials or fixed assets, but not more than half should be of that nature. It is always preferable to have the whole sum available in cash. It obviously remains an asset of the company and can be used for the company's business. Most banks will agree to allow an overdraft for a sum equivalent to the amount which has been deposited with them, but the capital must be seen to exist. It must therefore be placed in the business's bank account. You cannot just say: 'I have the money available.'

You need at least two and not more than 50 shareholders. An SARL does not have directors in the British sense: there is no board of directors. The company is represented officially to the outside world by a manager, *un gérant*. There can be two or three *co-gérants*, each one able to commit the company as regards third parties. Even though the internal rules demand the agreement of all the *co-gérants*, this has no effect if the third party was not aware of these rules.

Companies must have a registered office, and be able to produce evidence that the address does exist: you must either be shown to be the owner of the property or have a lease. Many companies in France use an accommodation-type address, but this service costs a lot more than in Britain. The law concerning the address of a new company has recently been changed: during the first two years of a business's life you can use your own private address. In fact, many businesses continue, for several years, to use the private address of the *gérant* or of one of the shareholders as the registered office.

In Britain, all companies must have an auditor, irrespective of their size. In France this is not the case. Most SARLs, in their first few years of existence at least, will not need an auditor.

With a limited company, as in Britain, the profits are not considered the income of the shareholders. A company can pay salaries to its employees and to shareholders who are working for it and such salaries are treated as the income of these individuals. The company, if it has profits after payment of the salaries, is taxed to the equivalent of company tax.

Sole trader

The other way to set up in business is as a sole trader. In French, this is called *entreprise individuelle*. The registration formalities are simpler: you need to show that you have a minimum capital; you have to register, simply, with the various authorities, who will want evidence of address, date of birth and all the usual personal details. If you are a foreign national, you will very often need to have some documents translated into French, particularly birth certificates.

There are, basically, three different sorts of *entreprises individuelles*: the *profession libérale* (doctors, lawyers, accountants, etc), the *commerçants* (shopkeepers, traders), and the *artisans* (craftsmen).

From the legal point of view, a sole trader does not have the protection of limited liability if something goes wrong. The income from your business is treated as your own personal income and is therefore subject to income tax.

How social security payments may affect your decision

You must think carefully, when deciding between a limited company and the status of sole trader, about the social security consequences. France has a very highly developed system of social security, of which the French are justly proud. It is paid for both by employing bodies and by employees and covers retirement pensions, health insurance, family allowances, unemployment insurance, etc. The social security system is very bureaucratic, and there are many bodies to whom these subscriptions have to be paid. Someone who starts up a business as a sole trader must reckon, in his first two years of trading (where his income cannot yet be established), on paying fixed contributions of some 25,000 francs. After that, social security contributions will represent some 35 per cent of his total earnings before tax.

Even though your business may have no income at all – as is often the case in the first months or years of a new business – the French authorities insist that you pay this amount, so that you have social security coverage, come what may. The only way to avoid this is by showing that you are already paying these contributions in another country of the European Community.

In the case of a company, an advantage is that you can determine the salary you pay yourself and if necessary limit the amount in order to minimise the social security contributions. The disadvantage is that for a salaried person, the total contributions payable are significantly higher, around 60 per cent of the net salary you draw out of the business, in return for which you get higher benefits than if paying as a 'self-employed' person. In addition, it is necessary for a certain minimum salary to be paid in order to qualify for benefits.

Beware, however: if you are the *gérant* of the company and, together with your family, you own more than 50 per cent of the shares, you will be treated as 'self-employed' and will have to pay the corresponding contributions.

So you should get sound advice, before deciding what form your business is going to take, on the consequences from the point of view of social security. You can go to a *Conseil Juridique* or legal adviser. The various bodies mentioned previously will be able to help you to find the right counsellor.

Taxation

As regards personal income tax, people in France make an annual return in respect of their income of the previous year. This is then processed by the French income tax authorities' computer system, which produces their annual tax bill. People do not pay income tax on a pay-as-you-earn basis, though this will probably change in a few years' time. They pay it the following year on an instalment basis.

As far as businesses are concerned, the French system is a self-declaratory system. This means that the business makes a return of what it has calculated to be its taxable income. Provided there are no obvious errors in the tax returns, these are accepted by the tax authorities. The taxable income of a business is not agreed annually with the authorities as in the UK. However, the Revenue does have the right, and generally exercises this periodically for all businesses, to carry out an in-depth investigation into the tax affairs of a business covering a period of four years.

Companies are normally required to file their tax returns within three months of their year end date and also to pay tax on their profits on the instalment system. For the unincorporated business, the profits are taxed as part of the personal income of the proprietor.

There are two rates of tax on companies in France: 42 per cent if the profits are distributed to shareholders and 37 per cent if they are retained within the business.

There are, however, many advantages for new businesses in France, be they limited companies or individual traders. Provided the business is really new (ie it is not the subsidiary of an existing company, or branch of an existing business, or even a business similar to one already carried on by members of the same family), and with the exception of certain activities such as dealing in property and professional services, there is a complete tax exemption for the first two years of trading. This means that a self-employed person can be completely exempt from income tax in his first two years of activity.

Value added tax

The VAT system in France (*TVA*, or *taxe à la valeur ajoutée*) follows the same basic rules as in other European Community countries. The differences are that you cannot recover your tax in the same month as you incur it; you have to wait for one month, effectively financing the State for this period. This is an important point to bear in mind with any new businesses: they will need additional working capital to finance the VAT which they cannot recover for a month. In addition, recovery of certain types of input tax is restricted, in particular VAT on vehicles.

Except for very small businesses, all VAT returns have to be made monthly, and not quarterly as in Britain. VAT refunds are not received automatically. They have to be applied for specifically at certain dates in the year, and do not come through very quickly.

The most common rate of VAT in France is 18.6 per cent, which applies to the vast majority of goods and services. However, food products and hotel accommodation are subject to VAT at the 'reduced' rate of 5.5 per cent. A higher rate of 25 per cent applies to radios, TVs, hi-fi equipment, cameras, private cars (including their rental), perfumes, tobacco products and certain other luxury products.

If the annual net amount of VAT due, excluding any VAT

recoverable on fixed assets, does not exceed FF1350, then the business does not come within the scope of VAT. For practical purposes, this means that all businesses in France are subject to VAT.

Other taxes relating to small businesses

France has many small taxes which do not, in themselves, raise a lot of revenue; however, returns still have to be made for them. There is, for instance, a tax on company cars. It is advisable, therefore, for a limited company not to have a company car on its books but rather for the owner or the shareholders to run their own personal cars and receive a mileage allowance. Other taxes are based on the amount of salaries paid in respect of apprenticeship training, further professional training, housing tax, etc, which could apply to certain businesses. In most big cities, there is a transport tax, representing between 1 and 2 per cent of salaries.

The banking system

Opening an account is covered in Chapter 6. Those who use their account for business purposes may find the bank services are less responsive to their needs than is the case in Britain.

A particular point to bear in mind is that businesses are still financed to a large extent by bills of exchange (*traites*). It is very common for businesses to send a bill of exchange on all their invoices for acceptance by their customer. Discounting the bill of exchange is then used by a business to raise short-term finance. This means that there are many million bills of exchange in circulation within the banking system. The system has to be geared up to handle all this paperwork, which exceeds the number of cheques.

Cheques are, of course, increasingly used in France. However, it is considered a very serious fault if you issue a cheque which you cannot meet. The first time a cheque 'bounces' on your account, you are given one month in which to put things right, ie give the bank proof that you have paid the bill to which the cheque referred. If you cannot produce that evidence, then you go on to the Bank of France blacklist and are not allowed to use a cheque book for one year. The only way you can then effectively make payments is by using bank transfers. Should a second cheque bounce, you are no longer given the chance to put things right and you automatically go on to the blacklist.

In France, bank managers, and certainly those in local branches, do not necessarily have much power to take decisions. You may well think that you are going to receive a favourable answer from a bank manager, not realising that he is, in fact, unable to take the final decision about your case; he has to refer to a regional head office where you will not be known personally and cannot expect the same personal consideration.

There is generally a certain reluctance, which is bred into the system, for people to take initiatives or decisions. This is changing more and more as France is becoming exposed to international business, but it will take some time before the system is radically altered.

Employee protection

Employees in French companies have a high level of job security. If a company wishes to cease employing someone for reasons other than obvious incompetence or dishonesty, it can be very difficult for it to terminate that person's contract. It can also prove quite expensive.

It is therefore essential for any business, when taking on a new employee, to do so for a trial period. The length of this trial period will vary, depending on the nature of the work, but make sure it lasts long enough for you to be able to assess the competence of the person employed. If you do not make it clear at the end of the trial period that you don't wish this person to remain in your employ, it will be assumed that you want to keep him and the contract will automatically become permanent.

When it comes to social security contributions, companies should reckon on paying an additional 40 per cent of the employees' salaries (some 45 per cent for executive personnel and senior employees). However, there are schemes available at the moment to encourage new businesses to take on staff. Small businesses often take on their first employee for a two-year period without having to pay the greater part of these charges (some 10 per cent only, instead of 40 to 45 per cent).

Buying property for business purposes

It is now common practice in France for businesses, particularly the smaller ones, to separate the property they own from the business itself. Property companies are very often set up, in the form of a *Société Civile Immobilière*, or *SCI* and these are the owners of the property. They then rent it to the business. The advantage is that if the business does not work out, the property itself remains in the ownership of the *SCI*, which will not necessarily be affected by the failure of the other company. In addition, if for any reason, you decide to dispose of the business, you do not have to dispose of the property at the same time. You can continue to draw an income from the lease of the property to whoever purchases your business. It is also an advantage for the tenant, as it reduces the amount of initial capital required to take over your business.

With an *SCI*, you do not have the protection of a limited liability company. As a civil company, the *SCI* cannot carry on a strictly commercial activity (the letting of the property is not considered to be commercial). The income from the lease of the property is considered as the shareholders' personal income and therefore taxed as such.

Dos and Don'ts

Do

Learn to speak some French.

Think carefully about exactly what you are looking for, where and how much you want to pay.

Give yourself enough time when you are house-hunting. A weekend will almost certainly not be enough.

Allow plenty of time to complete your transaction – especially if you are seeking finance for it.

Comply to the letter with your obligations under any *conditions suspensives* in the contract, particularly in relation to an application for finance.

Ensure, when seeking a loan, that you put in your application very quickly and have up-to-date financial information readily available.

Remember that exchange rates fluctuate.

Remember that the additional costs of purchase are high (up to 20 per cent).

Open a French bank account.

Allow plenty of time (not less than 15 days) for the transfer to France of funds, which must reach the *notaire* on or before the agreed date for completion, otherwise you may incur penalties.

Remember that French inheritance laws are different from those in the UK. Therefore, think about how you will structure the ownership of your French property.

Take advice, if a group purchase is envisaged, as to whether it should be in the names of individuals or a company.

Make a will.

Keep the *notaire* in the picture.

Take independent advice, particularly on the preliminary contract and, in the case of a multiple ownership development, the *règlement de copropriété*. Translation is not enough – it might not tell you the full legal implications of the documents.

Inspect your property thoroughly before committing yourself, especially when making stage payments on new buildings.

Check the boundaries of your future property against the Land Registry map obtainable from the *mairie* or through the local estate agent.

Make your preliminary agreement subject to local planning search.

Ask for a search of local motorway projects; there is a considerable road building programme in France, not to mention the high speed train (*TGV*).

Have documents checked by an expert before completion.

Obtain a *carte de séjour* if you are going to reside in France.

Have proper medical cover.

Remember to make sure that your pets are vaccinated and covered by a health certificate.

Remember that social security contributions are expensive and must be regarded as part of the taxation system.

Be aware, if you are setting up in business, that the French have a high notion of quality and expect a high degree of service.

Join in the life of your new community.

Do not

Sign any document before you have understood it or had time to take advice.

Sign any documents that have blank spaces 'to be filled in later', that have entries in pencil, or that are not dated.

Be overwhelmed by sales talk.

Buy from someone you chance to meet and who purports to be an agent. All estate agents in France have to be licensed and should have proper premises.

Pay any deposit to the vendor himself – only to a properly accredited agent or a *notaire*.

Under-declare the price.

Expect it to be just like it is at home.

Go overdrawn on your French bank account.

Forget to insure the property as soon as you complete.

Undertake any building or renovation work without adequate insurance, whether this is your own or the builder's.

Order renovation work from a chance acquaintance, who claims to be a builder, even if he is British. Builders have to guarantee their work for ten years and this means being properly registered.

Start any renovation work without first finding out if you need planning permission.

Start long-term renovations yourself unless you are confident you will have the time to see them through.
Over-estimate your building skills.
Under-estimate the building cost.
Forget that any income derived from your property in France must be declared to the French inland revenue as well as in the UK (subject to double tax treaty).

Bibliography

Buying Residential Property in France, Chambre de Commerce Française de Grande-Bretagne. Available from the French Chamber of Commerce, Knightsbridge House, 197 Knightsbridge, London SW7 1RB.

French Housing, Laws and Taxes, Frank Rutherford, Sprucehurst
Living in France Today, Philip Holland, Hale
Setting Up In France, Laetitia de Warren and Catherine Nollet, Merehurst
Your Home in France, Henry Dyson, Longman
The above publications are available from good booksellers.

Audio cassette and handbook: 'Your Property in France', New Agenda Productions. (For information ring 0822 853551.)

Various magazines, including *Homes Overseas, Resident Abroad, Homes Abroad, International Property Times, French Living, Housefinder in France* (Indicateur Bertrand), *Lagrange Anglais, French Property Buyer.*

Michelin Green Guides on the French regions.

The Holiday Which? Guide to France, Adam Ruck, Consumers' Association and Hodder & Stoughton.

Further Reading from Kogan Page

Buying and Renovating Houses for Profit, 2nd edition, K Ludman and R D Buchanan, 1988
Buying and Selling a House or Flat, Howard and Jackie Green, 1988
How to Buy and Renovate a Cottage, Stuart Turner
Living and Retiring Abroad: The Daily Telegraph Guide, Michael Furnell, annual
Working Abroad: The Daily Telegraph Guide, Godfrey Golzen, annual

Useful Addresses

General

French Consulate General, 21 Cromwell Road, Kensington, London SW7 2DQ; 071-581 5292

French Consulate General in Edinburgh, 7–11 Randolph Crescent, Edinburgh EH3 7TT; 031-225 7954

French Consulate General in Liverpool, 523–535 Cunard Building, Pier Head, Liverpool L3 1ET; 051-236 8685

French Consulate General in Jersey and Guernsey, Philip Le Feuvre House, La Motte Street, St Helier, Jersey; 0534 26256

French Embassy - Cultural Services, 23 Cromwell Road, London SW7; 071-581 5292

French Government Tourist Office, 178 Piccadilly, London W1V 0AL; 071-491 7622

Maison de la France, 8 Avenue de l'Opéra, 75001 Paris; 010-33 1 42 96 10 23 (French Tourist Office in Paris)

British Consulate General in Bordeaux, 15 Cours de Verdun, 33081 Bordeaux; 010-33 56 52 28 35

British Consulate General in Lille, 11 Square Dutilleul, 59800 Lille; 010-33 20 57 87 90

British Consulate General in Lyon, 24 Rue Childebert, 69288 Lyon; 010-33 78 37 59 67

British Consulate General in Marseille, 24 Avenue du Prado, 13006 Marseille; 010-33 91 53 43 32

British Consulate in Paris, 16 Rue d'Anjou, 75008 Paris; 010-33-1 42 66 91 42

British Embassy, 35 Rue du Faubourg St Honoré, 75383 Paris Cédex 08; 010-33-1 42 66 91 42

British Institute/British Council, 11 Rue Constantine, 75007 Paris; 010-33-1 45 55 95 95

Department of Social Security, Overseas Branch, Newcastle upon Tyne NE98 1YR; 091-285 7111

Ministry of Agriculture, Fisheries and Food, Animals Health Division, Hook Rise South, Surbiton, Surrey KT6 7NF; 081-337 6611

Property

Association Nationale pour l'Information sur le Logement (ANIL), 2 Boulevard St Martin, 75010 Paris; 010-33-1 42 02 05 50. This organisation will provide addresses of its branches in each *département*. For advice and literature on all problems concerning property.

Centre d'Information Logement, 204 Rue Lecourbe, 75015 Paris; 010-33-1 45 31 14 50

Fédération Nationale des Agents Immobiliers et Mandataires (FNAIM), 129 Rue du Faubourg St Honoré, 75008 Paris; 010-33-1 42 25 24 26

National Association of Estate Agents, 21 Jury Street, Warwick CV34 4EH; 0926 496800

Rutherfords, The French Agents, 7 Chelsea Manor Street, London SW3 3TW; 071-351 4454

Syndicat National des Professionnels Immobiliers (SNPI), 91 Rue de Prony, 75017 Paris; 010-33-1 42 27 82 05

Building

Compagnie Nationale des Experts Immobiliers, 11 Villa Brune, 75014 Paris; 010-33-1 47 66 65 39

Ordre des Architectes, 140 Avenue Victor Hugo, 75116 Paris; 010-33-1 45 22 20 27

Ordre des Géomètres Experts, 40 Avenue Hoche, 75008 Paris; 010-33-1 45 63 24 26

Banks

British banks with branches in France: Barclays, Lloyds, Midland, National Westminster (International)

Banque Nationale de Paris, 'Key to France', 60 Brompton Road, London SW3 1BW; 071-823 8994

Capital Home Loans Limited, 60 Gracechurch Street, London EC3V 0ET; 071-626 1043

CIC Groupe-Banque Transatlantique, Representative Office, 103 Mount Street, London W1Y 5HE; 071-493 6717

Crédit Agricole, London Branch, Condor House, 14 St Paul's Churchyard, London EC4M 8BD; 071-248 1400

Crédit Lyonnais, UK Main Office, PO Box 81, 84–94 Queen Victoria Street, London EC4P 4LX; 071-634 8000

Société Générale, London Branch, 60 Gracechurch Street, PO Box 513, London EC3V 0HD; 071-626 5400

UCB Group plc, Greenview House, 5 Manor Road, Wallington, Surrey SM6 0UX; 081-773 3111

Legal

Centre d'Information des Notaires, 1 Boulevard de Sebastopol, 75005 Paris

Conseil Supérieur du Notariat, 31 Rue du General Foy, 75008 Paris

Pannone Blackburn, Solicitors, 123 Deansgate, Manchester M3 2BU; 061-832 3000

De Pinna, Scorers & John Venn, 3 Albemarle Street, London W1X 3HF; 071-409 3188

Business

Department of Trade and Industry, Exports to Europe Branch, 1 Victoria Street, London SW1H 0ET; French Desk 071-215 5197

ESPACE, 2 Rue Ducourble, 59800 Lille (Training organisation)

French Chamber of Commerce (Chambre de Commerce Française de Grande-Bretagne), Knightsbridge House, 197 Knightsbridge, London SW7 1RB; 071-225 5250

French Industrial Development Board, 21–24 Grosvenor Place, London SW1X 7HU; 071-235 5148

Franco-British Chamber of Commerce, 8 Rue Cimarosa, 75116 Paris; 010-33-1 45 05 13 08

Messager, Jenkinson, Lebon, Business Lawyers, 20 Avenue du Peuple Belge, 59800 Lille; 010-33 20 55 29 39

Norman Smith, Accountant, 18 Avenue du Peuple Belge, 59800 Lille; 010-33 20 55 68 39

Glossary

Acompte. Down payment on a sale. The word itself is not legally binding. That depends on the conditions laid down in the contract when the down payment is made. Can apply to the sale of anything, whether property or object.

Acte authentique de vente. Final contract, signed on completion, drawn up and witnessed (or 'authenticated') by a *notaire*.

Acte de prêt. Loan agreement.

Acte sous seing privé. Private signed agreement between two parties, without the presence of a *notaire*. The pre-contract, if signed through an estate agent, is an *acte sous seing privé*.

ADIL. Association Départementale d'Information Logement. District Information bureau on housing. Can be consulted free on all aspects of local property purchase or rental.

Agent immobilier. Estate agent.

Aménager. To convert.

Ampoule. Light-bulb.

Appliqué. Wall bracket.

Architecte. Architect. *Architecte des Bâtiments de France.* Architect responsible for the granting of a building permit, especially in a listed area.

Ardoises. Slates.

Arrhes. A legally binding deposit, paid on account by the purchaser, on signing a contract. In the case of a property, it is not refunded if the purchaser backs out; if the vendor backs out, he owes the buyer double the deposit amount.

Ascenseur. Lift, elevator.

Assurance. Insurance. *Assurance-vie.* Life insurance. *Assurances multi-risques.* Comprehensive insurance.

Autoroute. Motorway.

Avocat. Solicitor, lawyer.

Bail. Lease contract between owner and tenant. *Bail emphytéotique.* Long lease.

Banlieue. Suburb.

Bâtiment. Building.

Bricolage. Do-it-yourself.

Bureau des Hypothèques. Property and Land Registry office, where the *notaire* deposits a copy of the sale contract, available for all to see.

Cadastre. Town planning registry.

Canapé. Sofa.

Carnet de santé. Health book. Issued at birth to every French child. All details concerning the child's health are entered in this book.

Carreaux, carrelage. Tiles (on floors or walls).

Cave. Cellar.

Centre commercial. Shopping centre.

Certificat d'urbanisme. Housing authorities' certificate detailing any public modification or construction project affecting a property in the process of being sold. Obtained by the *notaire* during his search.

Certificat médical. Medical certificate.

Chambre. Bedroom.

Charges. Service charges.

Chauffage. Heating. *Chauffage central.* Central heating.

Chéquier. Cheque book.

Clause suspensive. Condition outlined in a preliminary contract that must be satisfied for a sale to be completed. Otherwise, the buyer gets his deposit back.

Commissariat. Police station (in a town).

Compromis de vente. Preliminary contract signed by vendor and purchaser of a property, whereby the one undertakes to sell and the other to buy. In a *compromis*, if a buyer backs out of the sale, he cannot get another purchaser to take his place.

Compte courant. Current account.

Compteur. Meter.

Congélateur. Freezer, deep-freeze.

Conservation des Hypothèques. Land Charges Registry.

Constructeur. Builder. *Entreprise de construction.* Building company.

Co-propriété. Co-ownership (condominium in the USA). When owners of an apartment or a house on an estate share the property and responsibility of the parts available for common use (lift, stairs, roof, etc).

Court-circuit. Short-circuit.

Cuisine. Kitchen.
Cuisinière. Cooker.

DDAS. Direction Départementale de l'Action Sanitaire et Sociale. Hygiene and social services district office. Responsible for granting the right to install any exterior equipment connected with hygiene and sanitation (eg septic tank).
DDE. Direction Départementale de l'Equipement. District supplies office. Responsible for granting building permits, together with the *Architecte des Bâtiments de France*, on receiving application through the local *maire*.
Déclaration de revenus. Income tax return.
Déduction. Rebate (used mainly in fiscal terms).
Démenagement. Removal.
Dépendances. Outbuildings.
Devis. Estimate.
Disjoncteur. Circuit breaker.
Domicile principal. Main residence.
Domicile secondaire. Holiday residence.
Douane. Customs.
Droit de passage. Right of way.
Droit de mutation. Transfer duty.
Droit de Préemption. Pre-emptive rights, ie official right of precedence of one buyer (usually a local authority) over another.

Eau. Water. *Eaux-vannes.* Sewage water.
Ebéniste. Cabinet-maker.
Ecole. School. *Ecole privée.* Private, fee-paying school. *Ecole publique.* State school.
EDF. Electricité de France. Electricity board.
Electro-ménager. Household electrical goods.
Eléments de cuisine. Kitchen units.
Enduit. Coating, plastering.
Enregistrement. Registration.
Entrepreneur. Contractor.
Escalier. Stairway.
Essence. Petrol.
Etat des lieux. Description of a property, within and without, usually accompanying a lease contract between owner and tenant.

Fauteuil. Armchair.
Fenêtre. Window. *Porte-fenêtre.* French window.
Ferme. Farm. *Fermage.* Rent paid by a tenant-farmer.

Fiche. Plug.
FNAIM. Fédération Nationale des Agents Immobiliers et Mandataires. Estate agents' guild and financial guarantor.
Fonds. Funds. *Fonds de commerce.* Stock contained within a commercial property.
Forfait. Lump sum.
Fosse septique. Septic tank.
Four. Oven.
France Télécom. French National Telephone Company.

Gardien. Caretaker.
Gazinière. Gas cooker.
GDF. Gaz de France. French Gas Board.
Géomètre. Land surveyor.
Gérant. Manager.
Grande surface. Shopping mall.
Grange. Barn.
Grenier. Attic.

Héritage. Inheritance. *Héritier.* Heir.
Hypothèque. Mortgage. Mainly when a property is used as security for a debt. *Un prêt hypothécaire.* A mortgage loan.

Immeuble. Apartment building; in legal terms, simply a building.
Immobilier. Real estate
Impôt. Tax.
Indivision. Joint ownership of land or property.
Interrupteur. Switch.
Inventaire. Inventory.
ISF (*impôt de solidarité sur la fortune*). Wealth tax.

Jardin. Garden. *Jardinier.* Gardener.
Jouissance (droit de). Right of tenure.

Lampe. Free-standing lamp.
Lettre recommandée. Registered letter.
Livret de famille. Family booklet. Contains official notice of marriage, birth of children, deaths, divorce of a couple.
Location. Lease, rental.
Lotissement. Housing estate.
Lustre. Chandelier.

Magasin. Shop.

Maire. Mayor. A very important figure in French local life. Any request for a building or works permit must be submitted to him in the first instance.
Mairie. Town hall.
Maison. House.
Mandat. Mandate giving an agent the right to sell a property or, when coming from a prospective buyer, the right to look for a property. In general terms: power of attorney.
Maquette. Mock-up, scale model.
Marchand de biens. Land or property agent. Buys and sells property.
Médecin. Doctor.
Menuisier. Carpenter.
Meubles, mobilier. Furniture.
Minitel. Computer-based telephone information system.
Mitoyen. Party, neighbouring. *Mitoyenneté.* Common ownership of any object (wall, fence, etc) between two properties.
Moquette. Wall-to-wall carpet.
Mutuelle. Private health insurance.

Nettoiement (service du). Garbage collection.
Notaire. Notary. Public officer appointed and controlled by the Ministry of Justice. No property transaction is legally valid if it has not been witnessed and countersigned by a *notaire*. The *notaire* is also, more generally, a legal adviser.

Occupation. Occupation of premises. Also, profession.
Ordre. Order, association of members of the same profession or guild (*Ordre des Avocats*, *des Médecins*, etc).
Ordures. Rubbish.
Outils. Tools.

Parquet. Wood-block floor.
Patrimoine. Personal estate.
Pavillon. Bungalow.
Péage. Toll.
Pelouse. Lawn.
Permis de construire. Planning permission.
Pièce. Room.
Piscine. Swimming-pool.
Plomb. Lead. *Essence sans plomb.* Lead-free petrol.
Plombier. Plumber.
Plus-value. Capital gain.
Police d'assurance. Insurance policy.

Porte. Door. *Portail.* Garden door.
POS (plan d'occupation des sols). Official plan of the area.
Préavis. Advance notice.
Prise de courant. Electric plug or socket.
Promesse de vente. Preliminary contract on the sale of a property, whereby the vendor 'promises' to sell. If the buyer cannot complete, it is legally possible for him to find a substitute purchaser.
Promoteur immobilier. Property developer.
Propriété. Property.

Quartier. District, neighbourhood.
Quincaillerie-droguerie. Hardware store.
Quote-part. Proportional share in an acquisition.
Quotité. Quota.

Radiateur. Radiator.
Réfrigérateur. Fridge.
Rénover, Restaurer. To renovate, to restore.
Retraite. Retirement. Pension.
Rideau. Curtain.
Robinet. Tap.
Rocade. Ring road. (*Boulevard périphérique.* Paris ring road.)

SAFER. Société Aménagement Foncier et d'Etablissement Rural. Organisation entitled to exert pre-emptive rights on the acquisition of farms or farmland.
Saisie. Foreclosure.
Salle de bains. Bathroom.
Salon. Sitting Room. *Salle de séjour.* Living-room.
SCI. Société Civile Immobilière. Civil real-estate company. Formed by several people sharing the acquisition of a property.
Sécurité sociale. Social security.
Servitude. Charge on a property (eg a right of way).
Siège. Car seat.
Siège social. Business headquarters.
Sous-sol. Basement.

Taxe d'habitation. Rates.
Taxe foncière. Land tax.
Terrassement. Digging (for major works).
Testament. Will.
Toit. Roof.
Tout-à-l'égout. Main drainage.

Traite. Bill of exchange.
Tuiles. Tiles (on a roof).

Urbanisme. Town-planning.
Usufruit. Life interest (in a property).

Vaisselle. Crockery.
Variateur. Dimmer.
Viabiliser (un terrain). To make land available, ie to link it to water and electricity facilities.
Viager. Life annuity in a property.
Vitre. Window-pane.
Voirie. Municipal garbage-dump.
Voisin. Neighbour. *Voisinage.* Neighbourhood.

Zone classée. Listed area.

Index of Advertisers